EMPOWERED BY CONSCIOUSNESS

Connect with Your Inner Power and Create A Fulfilled Life of Abundance and Purpose

BY
JASON MEDLOCK

Copyright © 2023 by Expansion of Consciousness Incorporated

All rights reserved. No part of this book may be reproduced or used in any manner without written permission of the copyright owner except for the use of quotations in a book review. For more information, contact: info@jasonmedlock.com.

ISBN Paperback: 979-8-9890056-1-1
ISBN Electronic: 979-8-9890056-0-4
Library of Congress Control Number: 2023916420

Published in the United States of America by Expansion of Consciousness Inc.

Jason Medlock
Expansion of Consciousness Inc.
www.JasonMedlock.com

The publisher and the author are providing this book and its contents on an "as is" basis and make no representations or warranties of any kind with respect to this book or its contents. The publisher and the author disclaim all such representations and warranties, including but not limited to warranties of healthcare for a particular purpose. In addition, the publisher and the author assume no responsibility for errors, inaccuracies, omissions, or any other inconsistencies herein.

Table of Contents

Acknowledgments vii

Jason's Goals for This Book ix

Who This Book Is For xi
    How to Use This Book xi
    Maximize Comprehension: Tools and Strategies xii
    What Resources to Utilize Alongside this Book xiii
    How Long It Will Take to Put Modalities Into Practice xiv

Foreword xvii

Preface xix

Introduction 1
    Breaking Down the Matrix: Understanding the Illusion 1

Chapter 0: Spirituality 7
    The Nature of Reality 7
    Guidance 9
    Meditation to Connect to One or More of Your
    Spirit Guide/s 10
    Expanding Awareness 12
    Spiritual Modalities 14

Chapter 1: Meditation 17
    From Ancient Roots to Worldly Reach: The Evolution
    of Meditation 17
    Benefits of Meditation For Well-Being and Connection ... 18
    Embrace Stillness, Release Chaos 19
    Getting Started & Types of Meditation 20
    Steps for Your Meditation Practice: A Beginner's
    Guide to Inner Peace 21

Exploring the Depths: Common Variations to Enhance
Your Meditation Journey 22
Breathwork 23

Chapter 2: Manifestation 29
Pathways to Modern Manifestation: A Historical Journey 30
Exploring Manifestation's Scientific and Quantum Roots 31
Manifestation's Wide Spectrum of Benefits 32
Alchemy of Success 34
Alchemy Water Manifestation Technique 35
Keys to Successful Manifestation 38
Instruction 39
Where to Find More Information: Further Resources 41
Putting It into Practice: Embodying the Art of
Manifestation 43

Chapter 3: Hypnosis 45
Unveiling the Essence of Hypnosis 45
Connecting Ancient Wisdom with Modern Science:
The Story of Hypnosis 46
From Trance to Treatment: Hypnosis Unveiled by Science 48
Past Lives, Present Healing: Unearthing Insights Through
Regression 49
Hypnotherapy's Healing Power: Anxieties, Phobias,
and Addictions Unveiled 50
Journey into Self: Navigating Hypnosis for Transformation 51
Putting Hypnosis into Practice 53
Personal Past Life Regression Experiences 55
The Meditative Approach in Regression Therapy:
Understanding the Process 64

Chapter 4: The Third Eye Chakra and the Pineal Gland:
Gateway to Expanded Consciousness 79
The Pineal Gland 80
DMT 83
LSD 84
Mental Health Implications 85
Fluoride Exposure 86
Methods for Accessing the Third Eye 89

Breathing Exercises 91
Sunlight... 91
Yoga... 92
Sound Therapy 92
Crystals.. 93
Sleep 93
The Third Eye in the Animal Kingdom: Evidence
and Implications 94

Chapter 5: Deciphering the Psychedelic Experience: A Deep Dive into the Realm of Psychedelic Substances 99

Psychedelic Origins: Unveiling the Source of
Altered States 100
Reviving Psychedelic Research: A New Era for
Mental Health 102
Guidance and Safety: Navigating Psychedelic Experiences 105
The Two-Sided Coin of Psychedelics: A Balanced
Perspective 106

Chapter 6: Experiencing the Modality of Remote Viewing 111

The Controversial Journey of Remote Viewing:
Past, Present, and Future 111
Scientific Exploration of Remote Viewing: Targ, Puthoff,
and Swann 112
Where to Find More Information: Further Resources..................114
How Remote Viewing Works 115
ESP (Extrasensory Perception)..115
Practice Scientific Remote Viewing 116
Lost Dog Found Through Remote Viewing 117
Associate Remote Viewing 118
Exploring the Enigmatic Skinwalker Ranch Through
Remote Viewing 120

Chapter 7: The Art of Energy Healing 129

Reiki Energy Healing: Earth-Based
and Intuitive Approach 129
Galactic Energy Healing: Channeling Multi-Dimensional
Beings 130
Channeling the Energy..133

Chapter 8: Exploring the Subconscious Mind **135**
    What is the Subconscious Mind? 135
    Unveiling Ancient Subconscious Insights 136
    Subconscious and Unconscious: Revealing Differences 137
    Potential Benefits 139
    Unlocking the Power of the Subconscious Mind:
    A Journey to Success, Intuition, and Self-Discovery 140
    Elevate Your Mind for Success 141
    Further Resources for Deeper Understanding 143
    Empower Your Mind's Potential 144

Chapter 9: Channeling - Opening the Door to Higher Consciousness **147**
    The Foundation: Meditation and Centering 147
    Developing Your Channeling Practice 147
    Clearing Your Vessel: Preparing the Body, Mind,
    and Emotions 148
    Understanding Channeling from My Teacher Chloe Moers **149**
    Channeling Session "Live" with Jason Medlock 151
    Channeling Energy Healing Session 153
    The Foundation: Learning How to Consciously
    and Intentionally Channel 164

Chapter 10: The Wonders of Astral Projection **167**
    Astral Projection in Pop Culture and History 167
    Astral Projection Across the Ages: Exploring the History
    and Controversies of Out-of-Body Experiences 168
    Astral Projection: Personal Journeys, Skeptics,
    and the Power of Trust 171
    Unlocking Benefits of Astral Projection 172
    Journeying into Astral Projection: Preparation
    and Persistence 174
    Mastering Astral Projection: A Comprehensive
    Step-by-Step Guide 175
    Be a Lifelong Learner! 177

About The Author **179**

References **181**

Acknowledgments

I want to extend my heartfelt thanks to the remarkable individuals who made this book a reality. Your unwavering support, encouragement, and love made this journey possible. Primarily, I am grateful to my family, particularly my cherished sisters - Tareska, Toska, and Jocelyn. Your enduring belief in me, even when I was a curious young boy, provided constant strength during the writing of this book. Your unwavering support has meant the world to me, and I am grateful for every one of you.

To my old and new friends, thank you for standing by my side and cheering me on every step of the way. Your encouragement, late-night brainstorming sessions, and willingness to lend an ear have been invaluable. Your friendship and support have been a beacon of light.

I would also like to extend a heartfelt thank you to Chloe Moers, my spiritual advisor. Your guidance, wisdom, and belief in my abilities have been instrumental in shaping the direction and tone of this book. Your spiritual insights have given me the clarity and inspiration to explore the depths of spiritual modalities and share them with the world. From the bottom of my heart, thank you for being a guiding light on this incredible journey.

Finally, I express my gratitude to all those who have contributed to the field of spiritual modalities. Tony Sivalelli my Scientific Remote Viewing Instructor, David Wallace, my Associate Remote Viewing Instructor and Julia Cannon my QHHT instructor. Your dedication, expertise, and willingness to share your knowledge have been instrumental in shaping the content and message of this book. Your contributions have educated me and countless others seeking transformation.

Jason's Goals for This Book

With "Empowered by Consciousness," Jason sets forth several vital objectives. The primary aim is to recount his spiritual journey and wisdom, not as an end but as a resource for others. He envisions the book as a compass for those yearning to venture beyond the conventional boundaries of religious practices and delve deeper into varied spiritual modalities.

Jason's narrative serves as an open invitation to all readers, beckoning them to embark on their spiritual quests. Through recounting his exploration and the insights garnered along the way, he seeks to light the path for others and inspire them to chart their unique spiritual courses.

His stories and reflections intend to provoke thought and demonstrate the immense potential of awakening and manifestation. Jason knows these as powerful forces capable of initiating transformation and influencing our realities.

In essence, Jason aspires to have "Empowered by Consciousness" serve as a spiritual lantern - casting light on forgotten pathways, inspiring exploration, and illuminating profound power for awakening truth and manifestation. Within this book, he encourages readers to embark on their spiritual odysseys, discovering along the way the beauty of interconnectedness and the potential for personal transformation.

Who This Book Is For

"Empowered by Consciousness" is designed for the spiritually curious, the seekers of knowledge, and the explorers of the inner self. This book speaks explicitly to those who harbor a fascination with various spiritual modalities and wish to delve into the depths of consciousness.

It is a beacon for the open-minded, calling to those who crave personal development and growth. If you are intrigued by the mysteries of the universe and yearn to understand your unique role within it, read this book. It was created because of you, for you.

The beauty of "Empowered by Consciousness" is in its universal appeal. It doesn't discriminate between those steeped in religious traditions and those setting foot on the path of spirituality. It offers many insights and perspectives that connect with many readers, regardless of their spiritual backgrounds or the stage of their journey.

In essence, this book is a spiritual modality guidebook, an invitation to all willing to embark on a transformative journey of self-discovery, to learn of the cosmos and one's place in it, and to grasp the profound power of inner knowing and manifestation. It seeks to resonate with the spiritual adventurer in everyone, offering wisdom, guidance, and inspiration along the way.

How to Use This Book

"Empowered by Consciousness" is a conduit for personal spiritual journeys ignited by Jason's experiences and insights. The book's effectiveness, however, relies heavily on the reader's approach. Approaching the book with an open mind is paramount, as this paves the way for introspection and reflection - assisting spiritual remembering.

When reading, you are encouraged to engage with the concepts presented actively. Reflect on the themes, connect with your heart, and if they resonate, consider assimilating them. Jason's journey is not merely for passive consumption but an invitation for active exploration and participation.

This book further offers practical applications through suggested practices and spiritual modalities. Readers are encouraged to explore these practices at their own pace and comfort, treating each as a potential stepping stone towards personal spiritual growth. Remember, spiritual exploration is a personal journey, and there are no 'right' or 'wrong' paths - only the one that resonates for you.

In essence, "Empowered by Consciousness" is meant to be more than a book you read - it's a spiritual guide you interact with. It invites you to reflect, explore, question, and grow. Doing so aims to facilitate your navigation through the vast landscape of spirituality, helping you find your unique path and remember your place within the universe.

Maximize Comprehension: Tools and Strategies

To truly grasp the depth of insights in "Empowered by Consciousness," a proactive and mindful reading approach is recommended. Below are some strategies and tools to aid in the process:

1. **Reflective Reading:** Digest the book in chunks instead of rushing through it. Take the time to reflect upon the ideas presented, relating them to your own experiences, beliefs, and understandings.
2. **Journaling:** Maintain a journal to note thoughts, ideas, downloads, or questions that arise while reading. This process can aid with personal connection and spark new insights.
3. **Meditation:** Utilize meditation to deepen your connection to the book's concepts. Following a reading session, spend a few moments in silence to allow ideas to awaken and connect with your consciousness.

4. **Discussion:** Engage in discussions about your discovery with friends, fellow readers, or in book clubs. Exploring different perspectives can broaden your awakening.
5. **Practical Application:** Experiment with the spiritual practices and modalities suggested in the book. Practical application can provide firsthand experience and deepen comprehension.
6. **Revisiting Content:** Don't hesitate to re-read sections or chapters that are complex or particularly resonant. A second or third reading can often reveal more layers of meaning and resonance.
7. **Open-mindedness:** Maintain an open mind throughout. Even if some concepts challenge your existing beliefs, contemplate them rather than dismiss them outright.

Remember, awakening personal and universal truth is not a destination but a journey. Be patient with yourself and allow your comprehension to grow as you progress through the book.

What Resources to Utilize Alongside this Book

As you explore "Empowered by Consciousness," supplementing your journey with additional resources can be incredibly beneficial. Here are some suggestions:

1. **Related Books:** Expand your learning by exploring literature on metaphysics, spirituality, consciousness, meditation, and manifestation. These texts help build a more comprehensive foundation and offer varying perspectives on the subjects Jason discusses.
2. **Online Courses:** Many online platforms offer courses on spirituality, meditation, astral projection, and manifestation, among other related topics. These can provide structured learning experiences and practical techniques to add to the information you read from the book.
3. **Workshops:** Engaging in workshops can facilitate personal experiences, allowing you to practice and better awaken the spiritual modalities discussed in the book.

4. **Spiritual Communities:** Joining local or online spiritual communities can offer invaluable support. They can provide a space for discussions, shared experiences, and mutual learning.
5. **Podcasts and Webinars:** Many experts in the field host podcasts or webinars discussing a wide array of spiritual topics. These can provide contemporary insights and stimulate deeper thinking about the concepts introduced in the book.
6. **Guided Meditations:** Numerous guided meditations are available online, some specifically designed to assist in the practices of astral projection and manifestation. Guided meditations can offer practical guidance and aid in your personal remembering and awakening journey.

Each resource you engage with can add another layer of inner remembrance, enhancing your exploration of the rich landscape of spirituality and consciousness that is presented.

How Long It Will Take to Put Modalities Into Practice

Implementing the spiritual modalities discussed in "Empowered by Consciousness" is a highly individual process with no fixed timeline. The speed at which you progress will depend on several factors; including your commitment, openness, and consistency in practice.

Learning and incorporating spiritual practices requires patience and dedication. It's not a race but a journey of self-discovery and growth. Some may find specific modalities more accessible or resonant than others and may choose to focus on these first or foremost. Others may opt for a more comprehensive approach, exploring each modality.

It's essential to allow yourself ample time for exploration and learning. Be patient with the integration process - it can be as subtle as it is profound. Remember that spiritual development, like physical or intellectual development, isn't always linear and can involve periods of rapid growth and seeming stagnation.

Finally, it's crucial to approach these practices with a mindset of non-judgment and self-compassion. Every individual's journey is unique, and comparing your progress with others' may distract from your personal growth and discoveries. Embrace your path, honor your pace, and trust that with consistent practice and commitment, progress will unfold in its own time.

-Jason

Foreword

By Chloe Moers

Chloe Moers ~ Unconditional Love Reiki founder, Past Life Regression Therapist, Channeler, Galactic Energy Healing Master, Author, Interspecies Communicator, and Herbal Energy Healing founder.

Experiencing Jason's growth from a curious inquisitor to a skilled practitioner in many modalities has been a joy to experience. He first reached out to me, expressing an interest in channeling which ended up planting a seed that resulted in an abundant garden. After introducing and interviewing me on his podcast, *Expansion of Consciousness*, we began channeling sessions and classes and then progressed into his learning of Galactic Energy Healing.

Jason's determination and inspiration awakened opportunities for him, allowing for the chance of incredible practitioners and knowledgeable leaders around the world to teach him their wisdom.

It has been an honor seeing yet another seed sprout into a forest for Jason, this time in the form of a transformative book- one I highly recommend to anyone feeling there is more to life than what we see.

His sections on Remote Viewing, Past Life Regression, and Manifestation particularly felt fascinating to read with each chapter being significant in a web of wisdom.

May the information in this book awaken your heart, engage your mind, uplift your spirit, and aid you in releasing all that does not serve your greatest and highest good.

Preface

Empowered by Consciousness is an expansive chronicle that delves into Jason's compelling spiritual expedition and the gradual metamorphosis of his learnings and experiences. The book reflects Jason's life, beginning with a childhood steeped in the Methodist tradition. His early fascination with spirituality, captivated by the enigmatic and uncharted domains of the metaphysical, laid the groundwork for his ensuing spiritual exploration.

The narrative unfolds, chronicling Jason's journey of self-discovery and spiritual growth. From his nascent experiences in church - a beacon of his faith and a platform for his budding spiritual curiosity - to his maturing views on divinity, spirituality, and the vast cosmos, Jason's story is a vivid mosaic of his transformative path. This book isn't merely a recounting of experiences but a testament to an individual's evolution, fueled by a flowing curiosity and a powered quest for truth.

Delving into the realm of spiritual modalities, Jason shares his explorations and experiences. From the ethereal journeying of astral projection to the potent art of manifestation, the tranquility of meditation, and the profound connections with spiritual guides, he intricately weaves each element into a spiritual tapestry. Each modality, Jason explains, serves as a stepping stone on his path, imbuing him with new insights and deepening his understanding of the spiritual realm.

Jason underscores the profound interconnectedness of all life throughout his narrative, a concept central to his understanding of spirituality. He believes in the extraordinary power of inner knowing, its potential to shape reality and the capacity for individual transformation it holds. The journey he presents in "Empowered by Consciousness" serves as a testament to these awakened knowings, offering readers an insight into a spiritual voyage that is both deeply personal and universally relatable.

Introduction

Breaking Down the Matrix: Understanding the Illusion

I remember going to church every Sunday with my family as a child: sitting, praying, sleeping, and most of the time, playing with toys. Even as a nine-year-old, something about the weekly ritual didn't resonate.

I couldn't quite put my finger on it, but I found the entire process of going to church boring, and I remember asking my sister Jocelyn 10,000 questions. I would ask about the universe, the stars, and anything you could imagine that was beyond. I knew there was more to my existence than what the church implied.

Looking back, it is curious that a young boy would spend time thinking about his existence. Many young boys think about toys, playing sports, comics, movies, and collecting different *Star Wars* action figures, but I was contemplating my consciousness. I felt driven to know myself and my place in the world on deeper levels.

For instance, the Moon's orbital lock to our Earth—a strange phenomenon—was something I was *obsessed* with. I would stare at the moon and imagine how it traveled around the Earth while we were all orbiting the sun. It seemed unbelievable—and equally incredible—as it was so 'ordinary.' Now that I look back at it, I can say this (along with a few other discoveries) laid the foundation for my journey.

With my head full of ideas of cosmic and metaphysical musings, I would ask my mom, "Mom, why are those people shouting in church?" And I would ask my sisters, "Who is God, and where is he at?" I remember having a peculiar feeling that something wasn't right. I felt conflicted because I knew I believed in God, yet at this point in my walk, I was having a hard time wrapping my head around the idea of omnipotent power. But I was deep in wonder about it all.

Years later, I remember going home for the holidays, and we'd go to church on Sunday or for any special occasion. Even though I would sit in church with my mother as a young adult, I still never really felt that the church experience was for me. This feeling stayed with me even after my mother passed.

Something changed dramatically, however, when my sister Tareska introduced me to the affirmation of faith while attending the University of Nevada Las Vegas. The words in this affirmation changed the trajectory of my life. The experience of chanting my affirmation was incredible, even though I had no conscious clue what I was doing.

Later, I realized what Tareska had given me resonated in my soul as a form of metaphysics. The process did not take long, and soon I thought, "Oh my God, this stuff works." It just blew me away that words could have that kind of effect on me. By affirming my faith daily, I began to tap into my higher self, and when you do that, you tap into the frequency of giving, knowledge, and positive abundance. As a result, my third eye chakra began opening.

As I move forward, I look back at my journey to gain more perspective and share my insights and discoveries with others. In my 20s, I played college football; in my 30s, I was married and had kids, and then I spent my 40s rediscovering myself. Now that I have hit the 50 mark, I've discovered that our reality is not what I initially thought—and I guess that if you are reading this, you have had a similar discovery.

My approach has been discovery, research, remembrance, and practice. I understood that bringing an open and curious mind to things I did not understand would serve me, and this attitude allowed me to expand my consciousness. This practice is known as mindfulness. Being mindful is becoming aware of all the *small* things that occur in and around your life. I recommend adopting this mindset and researching any topic or subject explained in this book that interests you.

Stay open and curious and seek to back up your research with actual practice so that you can integrate what works for you and move on from what doesn't. After any documentary or seminar I attended, I found it helpful to do more research until I was comfortable with the information. Then, once I could understand and apply what I'd learned, the new insights would significantly impact my life.

I first read Elizabeth J. Womack's *Lessons from the 12 Archangels*. This book focuses on the origins of divine love, the creation of 12 Archangels, the story of the beginning of the earth, the illusion of time, and fear; this book catapulted me into my awakening. I can't recommend it highly enough.

Of course, I didn't stop there; I read *Angel Words* and *Healing Words from the Angels* by Doreen Virtue. These books focused on using high-vibratory words in your everyday language, which immensely helped with my vocabulary.

Later, I read *Journeys Out of the Body* and *Far Journeys* by Doctor Bob Monroe, and from those books, I understood that meditation is the key to having an out-of-body experience.

I also read *The Astral Projection Guidebook* by Erin Pavlina, which helped me experience my first out-of-body experience. Other books like *Forbidden Knowledge* by Jason Quitt & Bob Mitchell awakened my soul to several topics; including time travel, mind control, life in another body, crystal intelligence, and the untold story of Atlantis. There is a lot of valuable information in these books, and I needed time to ponder and explore them—and to practice what I learned.

The awakening process has been challenging at times. There were obstacles that I faced that forced me to see my ego literally. My heightened ego was a significant problem, and what I learned about myself eventually allowed me to go where I didn't think I could and feel many emotions I didn't know I could. This experience was both a blessing and a real challenge. In short, there were many things that I had to recognize and release to move into full awakening.

For instance, I had to become aware of how I spoke to people and examine the friends I was hanging around. Although they were good people, they didn't understand what I was experiencing once I was committed to my path of self-discovery. At times, I found myself in the wrong place at the wrong time; we all can attest to what struggles and challenges that can bring. I also found myself unable to deal with hard news appropriately. I needed to grow beyond my limiting self-concept to know the truth deeply and consciously. Without question, I had to release a lot internally to clear my vessel.

Now that I'm "awake," I can see everything for what it is (most of the time). I can see the spiritual awakening across our country and the differences between those who have begun to awaken and those who haven't. Amazingly, I can see our current matrix and how God has developed this cosmic plan for us all. And now that I consciously realized all our spiritual gifts, it's my calling to share the knowledge.

Here are a few things I've learned and will share with you: I've learned how to leave my body through astral projection. I've learned how to connect with meditation to help keep my mind still for hours; allowing me to manifest love, abundance, and increased intuition. I've used psychedelics to visit other realms and to observe the human ego. I've practiced seeking impressions about distant or unseen targets by "sensing" with my mind with the modality of Remote Viewing.

I've also studied energy healing modalities such as Reiki and Galactic Healing Energy. I felt called to experience both modalities, and the results were so excellent that I needed to become a Certified Galactic Energy Healer. In addition, I've learned how to channel multi-dimensional beings and healing energy through methods taught to me by my spiritual teacher, Chloe Moers.

I wrote this book for those who want to learn how to awaken their inner powers and use them for the good of themselves and others while incarnated here on Earth. We have so many different spiritual gifts, and expanding consciousness can help you and others discover our inner power.

I love researching spiritual experiences, whether others' or my own. On my podcast, *Expansion of Consciousness*, I've had the opportunity to directly interview many people worldwide who have experienced profound spiritual awakenings. These guests include mindset coaches, spiritual coaches, channelers, empaths, Reiki masters, Pleiadian Starseeds, mediums, remote viewers, and past-life regressionists. From those interviews, I learned that hearing people speak about their spiritual experiences can help expand their minds. Because of this, I felt called to open the blinds of a window into myself through my experience and insights.

We are all on unique journeys, but the sense of community and connection we get from sharing our knowledge and experiences are precious. We can learn much from each other and be inspired to go deeper. When I get asked, "How do you speak to God?" or "How do you reach God?" my immediate response is that the answers to those questions and others of that nature are inside us and all around us.

Empowered by Consciousness focuses on learning and remembering how to enhance your consciousness using spiritual modalities. Everything you want to achieve and anything you've thought you needed starts from within. I hope more people follow that premise because everything we see externally is a reflection. You start living when you explore what's within.

Chapter 0

Spirituality

In her book, *What Is Spirituality?*, Elizabeth Scott, Ph.D., asserts that spirituality "offers a worldview that suggests there is more to life than just what people experience on a sensory and physical level."

Spirituality encompasses all our extraordinary gifts, how to explore them, and what purpose they serve in our current incarnations. In short, there is a world beyond and within what we hear and see.

The Nature of Reality

Some believe humans have accomplished everything. They feel the world is a hologram; some call it a real-life matrix. I call it a *biological genius* with a high level of symmetry. Source has beyond infinite power that is expressed in our current reality and worlds beyond this one. Our soul is present here and in other realms unknown to us (consciously). Source ultimately is everything in everything and experiences all simultaneously in all dimensions.

You may have questions and doubts if this perspective is new to your current self. Explore and research with an open mind, and don't fear to unlearn and relearn. We can do that daily with books, movies, ideas, insights, and downloads to expand our awareness of the world. Without question, understanding experiences in different realms requires a certain level of focus and trust.

Souls can have an infinite number of incarnations in multiple dimensions and realities. I'm speaking of nine dimensions (although there are many more). Scientists have already discovered we are separated only by frequency from the next dimension. Our (physical) eyes don't see these higher dimensions, but people are capable of traveling to different dimensions using their consciousness, meditation, and even through astral travel.

Our spirits inhabit all nine dimensions as avatars and as energy. I've always imagined what it would be like to live on other planets as my soul has already lived there. Somehow, I know that there is highly evolved life on other planets in a way that transcends my current lifetime.

The more advanced we become, the more our consciousness expands, and the more we remember how to access the ability to change form. Highly advanced remembered beings can take whatever form they like. The benefit to this is to move through dimensions, like the one we currently live in (3rd dimension), to the higher vibrational dimensions. My goal is to move from 3rd-dimensional thinking and experiencing to 5th-dimensional living and experiencing. To ascend to higher dimensions, alignment with Source Love is necessary. Aligning one's vessel with this energy will speed up this transition process. If all this sounds far out, you are on the right track. It is.

I'm constantly learning—integrating new ideas and finding new meanings. I'm developing a broader perspective of life, traveling to different dimensions and physical locations with astral projection, meditating for calmness, understanding my past lives with regression therapy, analyzing the human ego by using psychedelics, and finally, using all the power within to manifest the life that resonates the most. It's an ambitious plan, but I know we can do great things, so I keep my horizons high.

Exercise Your Thoughts

Reflect on your current beliefs and perceptions of reality, unanswered questions, and potential areas of interest you would like to explore when embarking on this journey. Source is the beginning of life as we know it. All souls that incarnate are from Source as Source; in every dimension, every solar system, every galaxy or universe, all living beings are from Source, and with that knowledge, you begin to understand that we are all connected, just like a network.

Have you ever marveled at how the internet has networked people together? This awareness can be applied to the knowing that Source connects all souls. How we can communicate virtually with other people here on Earth is similar to how we can communicate with beings in different dimensions. Regardless of where you are in the universe, we are all connected.

Guidance

I'm a big fan of James Van Pratt (world-renowned psychic/medium). My experiences with my spirit guides strengthened the realization that I am never alone. Spirit guides are here to help us. You can speak to your guides while engaged in meditation and the dream state.

You might be wondering what precisely a spirit guide is. Chloe Moers; a channeler, intuitive, energy healer, past life regression therapist, and interspecies communicator channeled that, "a spirit guide is a consciousness, being, spirit, or essence in any form that is present to guide you in what is needed in any given moment. They may have lived in the body of a human once or may not have. Some even lived in the body of an elephant, ant, tree, or stone- or as beings beyond Earth life."

A spirit guide could be a family member; such as your mom, dad, sister, brother, or any loved one or person you have connected with (in this life or other lives). These guides are learning and growing with you, even though they are not here in material form. Sometimes family members or other-species companions (such as a dog) who have passed can connect with you as one of your spirit guides. When you have a family member for a spirit guide, what they didn't provide for you in the material world, they will do so now from the spiritual realm. It's important to note that spirits entirely awaken once transitioned (as we fully remember truth).

In addition to having guides of those we have known personally (in this life or other lives), people have spirit guides that are known through incarnations but through energy connection and necessity. We have spirit guides to assist us in developing our gifts, remembering who we are, releasing trauma, opening our hearts, and so much more. A spirit guide may assist us with one particular purpose or several. They can be called upon intentionally and specifically or opened and allowed to help on deeper levels.

I call on my spirit guides for help with all my goals, including my career (the one/ones who are there to assist with what you called for will be the one/ones to help). For all the spiritual modalities I speak of in this book, I call on the spirit guide/s that resonate for guidance at that moment.

Spirit guides can also be considered spiritual teachers. We all have a spiritual teacher available to us whenever we need them. Our guides inspire us with truth every day. We need them because, upon the incarnation, we forget much of who we are and need help to remember once again. Our spirit guides also help us decide what is necessary for the next incarnation. While in the spiritual realm, we commonly use our guides to heal, remember, experience joy, plan, and learn. Our guides are always there with and for us; we are never alone.

Have you ever felt the presence of your spirit guide(s)? Sometimes we hear people say they heard a voice speaking to them during a crisis. What is that voice? Sometimes, it's more of a feeling than words. When you call for various guides, you use your feeling (or impression) to distinguish what type of guide you are connecting with. Spirit guides, protect, and help us; they are here for us. Connecting with our guides reminds us of how we are all connected in the physical form and the spiritual form. We are all one source.

Meditation to Connect to One or More of Your Spirit Guide/s

Let's connect.

Lie down or sit in a chair comfortably and without distractions.

Relax your mind and be mindful of living in this moment.

As you become aware of the body, be mindful of your breath.

As you feel more aware, focus on the breath coming in through the nostrils, down into the torso.

As you become more aware, focus on the heart pumping blood through the body.

Take two deep breaths; imagine a beautiful light flowing from the skies into your crown chakra.

Please focus on the light; watch it expand into every part of your body, and watch it grow until it is outside the body and beyond.

Bring your awareness back inside your body and tell yourself that there is a beautiful spirit there.

Imagine light touching every organ, cell, and muscle in your body; imagine your body illuminated—Exhale with a count of 1, 2, 3, 4.

Inhale again with a count of 1, 2, 3, 4.

Exhale out of the mouth, dissipating all the ways of thinking that no longer serve you and releasing the limitations of the mind, exhaling fear out of your space.

Inhale beautiful purple light from Source, replacing the fear you exhaled.

Hold your breath for...1, 2, 3, and 4, and exhale out of the mouth.

Inhale again, hold for...1, 2, 3, 4; let it go, and exhale 1, 2, 3, 4.

Now you can open yourself up to spiritual beings. Imagine a beautiful garden area full of greenery that extends as far as the eyes can see—trees and flowers of all different colors, shapes, and sizes. Remember, you oversee creation now, so let it be what your heart wants it to be.

You come across a bench under a tree, emanating light and energy. Know that this bench connects you in a peaceful way. Imagine a being of light (Your Guide) coming close to you while you are seated. Invite your spiritual guide to come and sit with you.

Become aware of your guide's presence; be present and feel their feelings and energy so you can identify them. Trust yourself and your guide. Invite them to come in closer to you, and invite them to move through your chakras so that you feel their presence on a deep level. As they come in, speak to them with your thoughts and ask for your guide to share a message with you. Say, "Let me consciously receive your message at this time." Sit in silence and listen.

Thank this loving guide for being with you today and send them unconditional love energy.

Ask your guide to give you a sign whenever they are with you. Again, thank your guide, relax, and feel the love. Feel their love.

Inhale.

Exhale. Bring your awareness back to the body, back to your feet on the floor, back to your back sitting (or laying) against the chair, and back to your legs, arms, neck, and head.

Inhale.

Exhale. Slowly open your eyes. IT IS DONE!

You can use this meditation in a variety of ways. You can use it to connect with your spiritual guides, or you can use it to connect to another spiritual being. The feeling you receive should feel right and kind, and it is likely to feel very grounded, and many times you will receive a feeling of gratitude and love in return.

Expanding Awareness

Looking up at the night sky, the stars made me curious. I didn't understand what stars were and how they didn't appear to be moving. *Some are bright, some are faint, but they are everywhere.*

The universe is vast and full of energy, and this very vastness leaves us all wondering, *Are we alone?* The answer lies within the divine power of Source.

God sent forth this energy, sound, and light in the name of oneness and created the universe through manifestation. The universe comprises many particles capable of sensing each other because they are connected in love.

In *Lessons from the 12 Archangels*, Elizabeth Womack writes that the center of God's energy is the Central Soul, and all Creation originates from the Center Soul. When I first read Elizabeth Womack's lines about the Central Soul, it was revealed that God created the universe with beyond-infinite energy.

Source is all, and we all are Source. In my mind, I knew that "I was." I knew I was more than just a young kid with all these thoughts and experiences. I knew that I was part of a network of other spirits. Source has allowed us to experience life and the splendors of life ourselves. As a boy, I pondered the questions of existence while observing the skies and the vastness of the universe. I see that it all comes back to oneness.

When I thought of the universe as a young man, I wanted to know how it all started. It starts with energy, with love, with light and sound. We are surrounded by energy and live as energy. We are living within the entire universe of Source oneself. We are living as God in every being we meet in this multiverse.

Elizabeth Womack explains that God's energy moves out as a colorful spiral from the center with infinite rings of energy, sound, and light. The twelve Suns were created from the central sun, and these souls of God's energy came from all the galaxies and the stars.

God has always been my savior and my quiet place. Because I felt so comfortable with Source, I felt empowered to look deeper into what I was experiencing. I contemplated my surroundings in my development and still had many more questions. I knew I was on the right path. My calling was not to become a pastor but a researcher.

Spiritual Modalities

The abilities that human beings tap into from within are fascinating. Although it is human nature to explore ourselves and our surroundings, we are only beginning to remember how our internal landscape operates and how all people can use inner wisdom to improve their lives and the lives of others. This book is my contribution to this remembrance.

How would you like to awaken your inner capabilities? Your inner ability to design and create the life you were born to live? That is the overall theme of this book—how we can learn to develop the most profound aspects of our being and live more creatively and thoroughly.

I have always been fascinated with the unknown. I've read, researched, and attended seminars to increase my intuitiveness, and explored several powerful methods to program my subconscious mind—in some cases allowing me the ability to predict the outcome of future events, receive answers to my everyday questions, and locate objects that were previously unknown to my conscious mind. I always tell myself to stay inspired and focused to experience all that is for the greater good of all. To help you experience an expansion of consciousness, I felt it was important to share my experiences and how I figured out the best ways to integrate these teachings into my everyday life.

Let me provide some examples, though I will dive deeper into these and other concepts and modalities as we progress through this book.

You've heard of the Law of Attraction. I used this principle to attract people to me. I learned that the human body is made of light and sound and can tune our frequencies higher or lower. With the right frequency, you can attract anyone or anything in life to help you achieve your life purpose.

Associate Remote Viewing (ARV) and Scientific Remote Viewing (SRV) are excellent daily tools. I live my life with the ability to access my subconscious mind for answers to just about anything connected to the success of my clients or my personal life.

Meditating effectively is the key to continued success using these different spiritual modalities. Transcendental Meditation (TM) has changed my life. I've experienced physiological results like enhanced blood flow and increased oxygen levels, which allow me to think clearly at an expanded level of consciousness. I also enjoy a deeper sleep, can dissolve knots and tension, and am relatively stress-free. I now use TM in connection with everything else I do.

While experiencing transcendence, I've found that I can access my subconscious mind for all that I need, program my subconscious mind with affirmations, and have conversations with my higher self. I can also visit my spirit guides while in this state, communicate via channeling, and experience past lifetimes. I've connected with my higher self in many different settings, most notably in a trance with my spiritual mentor Chloe Moers.

Once I could quiet my thoughts using TM, I began to use Astral Projection to visit places I'd never seen; like Australia, Egypt, and the Florida Keys!

I've documented multiple conversations that I've had with the Collective via a medium, and these conversations have brought to light how we can live a fulfilled life while incarnated on Earth. The knowledge and wisdom I've gained from these experiences have significantly increased my awareness, intuitiveness, and energy.

I'm a certified Galactic Energy Healer, and I use this spiritual modality to heal myself and others. Connecting with energy from various dimensions can help you recover from various issues. This energy protects you from low energy. I also connect with this gift to send Unconditional Love Energy to humans and other species worldwide.

As you read more about these experiences and modalities in the following chapters, I hope that my experiences and study will inspire you to embark on your journey or to deepen the one you are already on. I have learned that expanding our minds through various awareness techniques can better create a life that resonates at the highest level. We better understand ourselves and the universe we exist in.

As I share these modalities, you can connect with them to enhance your life, as I am. However, your journey will be yours to flow with. In this way, I am simply your guide and an open door, and I encourage you to learn from what I have done while exploring on your own.

I feel full of love for all that I have learned, and I'm genuinely looking forward to an entire life of engagement with you as we all strive for love, light, and peace. May these pages bring you more than you believe is possible.

Chapter 1

Meditation

Meditation is the foundation for all of the other life-awakening modalities in this book. Meditation constitutes the backbone of all that I do, and if you can learn this valuable skill to experience your consciousness, it can catapult you to the next level of blissful existence.

Meditation involves the deliberate training of the mind and concentrated attention to gain mental clarity, emotional equilibrium, and spiritual remembrance. It is a profound journey of self-discovery and internal investigation that enables people to reach the depths of their awareness. Individuals learn to examine their thoughts and emotions without judgment through meditation, establishing a sense of peace and awareness.

Mindfulness is an aspect of meditation, as the process of quieting the mind can help us achieve a greater sense of conscious awareness in our day-to-day lives. Meditation is often paired with breathwork, a powerful tool for calming the nervous system and creating balance in the body.

From Ancient Roots to Worldly Reach: The Evolution of Meditation

The long history of meditation dates back thousands of years to the spiritual practices of ancient civilizations. Meditation first appears in texts such as the Vedas, one of the oldest, if not the oldest, religious works in the world, stretching back over 5,000 years to the Indus Valley. These works discuss many contemplative activities, including breath control, visualization, and the repetition of sacred mantras. Meditation was practiced in Hinduism as a path of self-realization and oneness with the divine and was essential to the teachings of ancient Indian sages and yogis seeking self-realization and freedom from the cycle of birth and death.

The rise of Buddhism in the sixth century BCE propelled meditation to the forefront of spiritual practice[1]. The Buddha attained enlightenment via prolonged meditation and shared his discoveries with his followers. Buddhist meditation techniques like mindfulness and loving-kindness meditation became essential to pursuing enlightenment and liberation from suffering. The spread of Buddhism throughout Asia aided in the popularity and diversification of meditation methods.

Meditation was equally crucial in other ancient religions. With its emphasis on nonviolence and penance, Jainism included meditation as a practice to achieve spiritual purity and enlightenment. Meditation was used in Chinese Taoism to promote inner harmony and harmonize with the natural flow of the universe. Eventually, meditation was released from (primarily) religious bounds and became a worldwide practice for anyone seeking personal progress, well-being, and inner calm. Meditation techniques became popular in the West in the late nineteenth and early twentieth centuries due to the teachings of spiritual leaders and scholars. This rekindled interest in meditation resulted in Western psychology and philosophy incorporating Eastern techniques.

Benefits of Meditation For Well-Being and Connection

Meditation is vital for anyone seeking holistic well-being and a greater awareness of themselves and the world around them. Research in the fields of psychology and neuroscience on meditation's effects and benefits has significantly increased recently.

---

[1] (https://www.indianetzone.com/28/date_upanishads_indian_philosophy.htm)

Regular meditative practices have been proven to reduce stress, anxiety, and depression, improve cognitive abilities (including attention and memory), and promote emotional well-being. Meditation has also been demonstrated to promote resilience, compassion, and social connection, as well as a sense of connectivity and empathy.

Neuroplasticity is the process by which the brain forms new neural connections. Meditation has been shown to change the brain's structure, remodeling the mind-body system on a cellular level for stronger interconnectedness.

The advantages of meditation go beyond mental and emotional well-being. Regular practice has also been linked to physical health benefits such as lower blood pressure, improved immunological function, and reduced inflammation[2].

Embrace Stillness, Release Chaos

The benefits of meditation are needed now. Our senses have been bombarded with constant stimuli in our daily lives: the constant TV noise, traffic, mobile notifications, and expanding to-do lists. Our thoughts have grown so accustomed to the noise that its absence feels almost strange. When was the last time you were engulfed in the profound tranquility of nature, far apart from the hustle and bustle of civilization? For many of us, when we do experience this occasional sense of quiet, it can be liberating but also foreign. Humans have lived in harmony with nature for longer than the mind can comprehend, and only recently have we become detached from this tranquility.

Unsurprisingly, stress, anxiety, and various other ailments have skyrocketed in recent years. These difficulties affect people of all ages. Keeping up with rapid technological improvements and maintaining job responsibilities, household chores, and social commitments might seem

---

[2] Benefits of Meditation | Santosh Yoga Institute. https://santoshyogainstitute.com/benefits-of-meditation

like an uphill battle for older people. Academic achievement, growing relationships, and setting one's career in the adult world can all be tremendously complex and discouraging for younger people.

The pervasiveness of social media has only worsened these issues, especially among the younger population. The constant flood of updates and notifications is a big distraction, and when kids compare their lives to the frequently unrealistic depictions they see online, it often creates feelings of inadequacy and self-doubt.

If you're feeling overwhelmed by the continuous barrage of information and sensations that modern life throws at us, you might be looking for a way to hit the pause and reflect button, giving your mind time to reset and revitalize. That's where meditation comes in. It's an easy-to-implement tool that can relieve the unnatural, fast-paced, and high-stress world many now live in. Coming back to loving awareness, returning to our true nature is the first step towards tapping into the great potential of our consciousness.

Getting Started & Types of Meditation

So, what is required to begin meditating? Not nearly as much as you might think. Amid the hustle and bustle of modern life, even 10 to 20 minutes of meditation daily can significantly positively influence your health and well-being, so set aside time to incorporate a meditation routine. Even taking a mindful walk is a form of meditation.

The next step is to connect with a form of meditation that resonates with you. As meditation has evolved alongside modern living, new techniques have emerged and been remembered. Individuals can connect with multiple methods based on their needs and goals. Some popular approaches include mindfulness, transcendental meditation, loving-kindness, and guided visualization. You can also find serenity through yoga, binaural beats, solfeggio frequencies, and even silent, contemplative prayer.

Guided meditation sessions are an excellent way to begin, with a soothing voice gently guiding you to relaxation and peace.

I want to spotlight **mindfulness**, as many people have found it particularly useful. Mindfulness is a meditative practice that emphasizes acute awareness of one's sensations and emotions in the present moment.

Steps for Your Meditation Practice: A Beginner's Guide to Inner Peace

Here are some basic steps to get started with your meditation practice.

1. **Settle in:** Find a quiet, comfortable place where you won't be disturbed during your meditation session. This could be in your bedroom, living room, or even a park or garden.
2. **Choose your position:** You can sit on a cushion on the floor, on a chair, or even lay down if that's more comfortable. The goal is to find a position that allows you to remain relaxed yet conscious. Ensure your posture is upright (or straight if laying) and your body is comfortable.
3. **Decide on the length of your session:** If you're a beginner, starting with just a few minutes each day can be a good approach. Over time, you can gradually increase this to longer periods, such as 20 minutes or half an hour (or longer).
4. **Close your eyes and breathe:** Close your eyes gently and bring your attention to your breath. Notice the sensation of the air as you inhale and exhale.
5. **Be mindful of your thoughts:** As you focus on your breath, you'll notice that thoughts may start to pop up in your head. This is okay. The goal isn't to stop or avoid thinking but rather to observe those thoughts without judgment, then gently bring your conscious awareness back to your breath- releasing these thoughts naturally.
6. **Use a focus aid (if resonating):** Some people find it helpful to focus on a word or phrase, known as a mantra, or follow a guided meditation (found on various apps or websites). This

can provide some structure to your meditation, especially when learning how to tap in through this body.
7. **Gently end your session:** When your chosen time is complete, slowly bring your conscious attention back to your surroundings. Take a moment to sit, keep your eyes closed, and be aware of where you are and how you feel. Then, open your eyes, stand up slowly, and stretch.

Exploring the Depths: Common Variations to Enhance Your Meditation Journey

Here are a few popular variations of meditation that you can incorporate into your daily meditation practice.

1. **Body Scan Meditation:** Start by focusing your attention on your feet and slowly moving your attention up through your body, having conscious awareness of each part of your body. Notice any sensations, tensions, or places of relaxation. Maintain a non-judgmental and curious mindset as you scan from your toes to the top of your head, noticing each area of your body.
2. **Loving-Kindness Meditation:** Begin by experiencing and encouraging feelings of love and compassion towards yourself. Repeat sentences such as, "May I be joyful. May I be healthy. May I live with ease. May I love fully with all of my being." After some time (or immediately if resonating), extend these well-wishes to others; first to a loved one, then gradually expanding to include neutral people, challenging people, and ultimately all beings.
3. **Walking Meditation:** Find a quiet location where you can stroll slowly and consciously (walking barefoot is recommended for grounding and mindfulness). Bring your focus to the sensation of your feet touching the ground, the movement of your legs, and the shifting of your weight. Notice any physical feelings and the surroundings around you. Allow yourself to be completely present at each stage.
4. **Breath Counting:** As you sit comfortably, count each breath cycle (inhale and exhale) from one to ten, concentrating your attention fully on the feeling of breathing. When you

reach ten, start again at one. If you lose count or your mind wanders, gently bring your attention back to the breath and resume counting.

Breathwork

Breathwork exercises, also known as pranayama in yoga, can be highly effective for calming the mind, reducing stress, and improving overall well-being. Here are some exercises you might find helpful:

Box Breathing

This is a simple technique where you inhale, hold your breath, exhale, and pause for an equal count (e.g., four seconds).

1. Inhale for a count of 4.
2. Hold your breath for a count of 4.
3. Exhale for a count of 4.
4. Hold your breath again for a count of 4.
5. Repeat the cycle.

4-7-8 Breathing

This method is often used for stress reduction and sleep improvement.

1. Inhale through your nose for a count of 4.
2. Hold your breath for a count of 7.
3. Exhale through your mouth for a count of 8.
4. Repeat the cycle.

Alternate Nostril Breathing (Nadi Shodhana Pranayama)

This practice is said to balance the right and left hemispheres of the brain.

1. Sit comfortably and close your right nostril with your right thumb.
2. Inhale through your left nostril.

3. Close your left nostril with your right ring finger and release your thumb from your right nostril.
4. Exhale through your right nostril.
5. Inhale through your right nostril, then close it, and exhale through your left nostril.
6. This completes one round. You can continue for as long as you feel comfortable.

Belly Breathing (Diaphragmatic Breathing)

1. Lay down or sit in a comfortable position.
2. Put one hand on your belly below your ribs and the other on your chest.
3. Take a deep breath through your nose, letting your belly push your hand out. Your chest should not move.
4. Breathe out through pursed lips as if you were whistling. Feel the hand on your belly go in and use it to push all the air out.
5. Repeat this breathing 3 to 10 times.

I encourage you to try out all of these breathwork exercises, as they serve different functions when paired with meditation. All you need to do is be a quiet place (if possible), take a deep breath, and begin the journey to a more peaceful mind and a healthier existence!

Always remember to practice these techniques in a calm, quiet environment, and make sure you're comfortable. It's also a good idea to consult with a healthcare professional before beginning any new breathwork routine, particularly if you have a respiratory condition or other health concerns.

Practice Makes Perfect

My mind was like a swarm of flies when I began meditating, flying from thought to thought. I learned to focus on my breath with the help of guided meditation and repeating mantras to help settle my thoughts. When my thoughts wandered, I noted them and gently brought my attention back to my breath. I could only focus for a few seconds at first, but with practice, I've been able to lengthen these intervals of mental clarity, substantially improving my meditation sessions.

Meditation has had a significant impact on how my consciousness empowers me. For example, I can now focus on my breath and rapidly calm myself at times of extreme tension. This increased self-awareness has also allowed me to realize my stress triggers better and create healthier strategies to handle them. Furthermore, it has enabled me to connect to a mental place of calm and clarity, from which I may resonate in anytime I need to.

So, take it from me, it's common to feel like your mind wanders more than it stays focused when you're just starting out with meditation. The key is to keep practicing regularly. Over time, you'll likely find that you can remain focused for longer periods and that you feel more calm and less stressed, both during and outside of your meditation sessions.

Meditation, like the other modalities we'll cover, is not only about gaining wisdom but also about actively participating in the experience and sharing the rewards with yourself and others. Meditation is a discipline that involves your personal participation and goes beyond theory.

Consistency is essential for putting meditation into practice. To experience the transformative benefits of meditation, developing a daily meditation regimen is critical. By dedicating time for yourself each day, you can build a deeper connection with yourself. Begin slowly, and progressively increase the duration as resonating.

Meditation does not have to be restricted to formal sessions. You can incorporate mindfulness into your everyday life. Try practicing awareness while eating, walking, or performing daily tasks. You may extend the advantages of meditation to your entire life by bringing present-moment mindfulness and nonjudgmental observation to all elements of your day.

It's vital to realize that meditation growth isn't necessarily linear. Along the road, challenges and unrest may occur. However, by being devoted to your practice and maintaining a caring and patient attitude, you can navigate past hurdles and continue to increase your connection and inner growth.

Embrace the phrase "doing, being, living." It is your invitation to actively engage in meditation and incorporate it into your daily life. You will experience and embrace the tremendous advantages of meditation by devoting time, love, and energy.

Remember, meditation is a personal practice, and it's vital to learn what resonates most with you.

Expanding Your Practice

To expand your meditation practice, consider reading books like *The Miracle of Mindfulness* by Thich Nhat Hanh or *10% Happier* by Dan Harris. These renowned experts offer practical guidance and deep insights into meditation beyond the scope of this book.

Additionally, websites like *Mindful.org*, *Headspace.com*, and the *Chopra Center* offer numerous resources, articles, and guided meditations for practitioners of all levels. These platforms are reputable sources, often curated by meditation teachers and experts, and can provide practical tips, techniques, and even online courses to deepen your meditation practice.

Podcasts have also become a popular medium for exploring meditation. *Insight Timer, The Meditation Podcast,* and *10% Happier with Dan Harris* are notable podcasts that feature discussions, interviews, and guided meditations led by experienced practitioners and teachers.

Furthermore, online communities and forums such as *r/Meditation* on Reddit or meditation-specific communities on Insight Timer allow you to engage in discussions, ask questions, and learn from fellow meditators. These platforms provide a supportive environment for sharing experiences, seeking advice, and connecting with learning individuals on their meditation journeys.

By exploring these resources, you'll find a wealth of information to deepen your practice of meditation. Remember to approach each source with an open mind and evaluate the credibility and relevance of the material to ensure a meaningful and enriching learning experience. May your intuition be your guide.

Chapter 2

Manifestation

Manifestation is transforming your thoughts, truths, and feelings into reality. It takes aspirations from your mind and heart and gives them life in the world you see. Manifestation begins with trust, feeling, and intention.

Manifestation brings anything into your current reality through thoughts, feelings, and visualization around your intention. Our beliefs shape our lives, and manifestation is the intention of bringing what's within to the outside world.

According to clinical psychologist and positive psychology expert Carla Manly, manifestation involves taking something you want and bringing it into reality. (Ref 1)

But manifestation can be positive or negative. Manifesting with the intentions of the greatest and highest good/love is essential. For instance, if you find a person you are attracted to and set to manifest them in your life (regardless of if they are good for you or not), this could be a very painful learning experience. That is why setting specific intentions is so important. An example of this intention could be, "I intend to manifest a person who is of the highest and most loving alignment with me to intertwine romantically if it is for the greatest and highest good/love of all."

How does manifestation work exactly? By mentally attracting a desired request in your direction, it can come to you because your focus is fully attuned to making it happen. We are powerful. If we can solely focus on the one thing we want, it will temporarily shift our energy and focus our thoughts on making that happen. Achieving our goals becomes much easier with manifestation.

Many have realized that we're all manifesting daily without consciously realizing it. (Ref 2) That said, if you want to receive more consciously intentional results from the practice, it's expressed that doing a manifestation technique is recommended. Manifestation is part of our nature. We have much influence on ourselves and our reality. Let's take a moment to explore the history of manifestation for better clarity on how intertwined it is with us.

Pathways to Modern Manifestation: A Historical Journey

The concept of modern manifestation goes back to 1906, when the term *Law of Attraction* was first coined by author William Walker Atkinson in his book "Through Vibration: The Law of Attraction in the Thought World." As he saw it, it is possible for humans to construct their reality through their thoughts.

Vibration and the Law of Attraction were controversial ideas then, and many wrote Atkinson off as being nothing more than a crazy man. But some realized the truth in his words, leading to the modern concept of manifestation in 1910.

It wouldn't be until 1928, a full eighteen years later, that someone else attempted to add meaningfully to the conversation. That person was Napoleon Hill, who penned "The Law of Success in 16 Lessons." That was one of many works he'd publish on the subject. Hill invested in the idea of manifestation and its power to help the world, and he continued to push the idea in his 1937 book "Think and Grow Rich," which eventually became a worldwide bestseller. There was a growing movement of people experimenting with manifestation.

Still, as much as the idea was catching on, it wouldn't be mainstream until 1986, when Jerry and Esther Hicks began carrying out first-hand research on whether there was any scientific validity to the concept. How did they do this? In a series of channeling sessions, they attempted to contact a nonphysical being named Abraham.

People started showing up to these seminars in droves as they saw something they'd been searching for their whole lives: hope! These events directly led to 2006, when Rhonda Byrne, a fan of Hicks' work, created a documentary film and a book named *The Secret*.

The Secret was an absolute phenomenon, with the book alone selling over thirty million copies worldwide. It succeeded because Byrne expanded upon the concepts of those who came before her and simplified them in a way anyone could understand. (Ref 3)

Following this, manifestation became part of the larger cultural conversation in a way it hadn't before. Manifestation is a widely discussed and recognized concept, leading many scientists to explore deeper.

Exploring Manifestation's Scientific and Quantum Roots

Some people may think of manifestation as a spiritual modality that many cultures have used for centuries, and there is science that validates its effectiveness. Recent studies show that positive thoughts can affect your physical and mental health and give you more control over your fears and stress triggers.

So, what are scientists working towards in this field of study, and what discoveries can we explore currently? While no universal scientific consensus exists, the results have confirmed that manifestation is real. As we mentioned earlier, if you can cut out the noise of daily life and instead focus your mental energies on the one thing you want, it can help you achieve it.

Is manifestation the placebo effect? That's what some people believe. The placebo effect is the phenomenon of experiencing positive results for a treatment or intervention with no active ingredients, and it can be positively impactful when used for treatment. Such a phenomenon has resulted in people getting better from low-level illnesses, even if the medication given to the patient shouldn't have any such effect. So, in a way, the placebo effect is an aspect of manifestation as it is founded on trust and belief.

Some people believe that manifestation has more to do with quantum theory. Quantum theory is the theoretical basis of modern physics and explains the nature and behavior of matter and energy at the atomic and subatomic levels. (Ref 11) My journey into manifestation has revealed that our thoughts and needs are projected into the universe and intertwined in quantum entanglement. This entanglement is full of data that vibrates at certain frequencies, and if you can raise your frequency to what you want, you will receive it here on Earth.

So, for those who practice manifesting daily, this would explain why the process works. They're channeling that desired frequency and using it to better their lives. After all, if the universe is indeed one interconnected energy and we're part of that, then the idea of someone briefly tapping into this quantum entanglement shouldn't sound absurd. (Ref 4)

Many channelers have shared information tapped into manifestation as well. "Imagination is Manifestation" (Ref 5) is a quote channeled by Chloe Moers to explain the process simply yet powerfully. In other words, to imagine is to create.

The scientific consensus on manifesting needs to be clearer and will likely become so. But while this continues to be discussed in the scientific community, many of those who practice it are receiving genuine results.

Manifestation's Wide Spectrum of Benefits

We've already touched upon some potential benefits of engaging in manifestation, but let's dive deeper as there is much to cover. For example, practitioners have noted that their overall positivity and optimism increase the more they manifest. Increased positivity is linked with improved motivation and goal-setting. If a person feels uplifted, the idea of transforming dreams into waking life flows easier. Manifestation techniques can be particularly beneficial for those who struggle with self-confidence issues, which can be common in the 21st century. It can also benefit those suffering from stress and anxiety, as studies have shown.

Through an increased ability to self-reflect and be self-aware, those who practice manifestation feel it can truly rewire the brain in an incredibly positive way. More direct observation of our thoughts, beliefs, and emotions makes overcoming obstacles much easier.

Now, this sounds like therapy to some, and, in truth, there are many similarities between the two as they both involve honest reflection and bettering oneself and one's life. The key difference is that manifestation is limitless and therapy is limited (depending on the skills of the therapist and the state of the client). A combination of both can also yield beneficial results to a potentially higher degree (depending on the person and situation).

In addition to what has already been shared, studies show practitioners have developed enhanced problem-solving skills, as practitioners access the ability to rewire the brain to change and improve while looking at the world in a better light. Aside from the emotional benefits, those who engage in manifestation have reported improved physical health, as the mind and heart strive for overall coherence. A positive mindset can improve the immune system overall. On top of that, manifesting has also been linked to lowering blood pressure, drastically being able to reduce the risk of heart disease and diabetes. (Ref 6)

Even if it may not solve all illnesses or conquer all of life's challenges, it can be, if used correctly, a very effective tool for personal growth- according to the many who now practice it regularly. With that in mind, we will look into how someone can easily practice manifestation.

Alchemy of Success

In the fall of 2020, a season that symbolizes change, my intellectual curiosity led me to explore alternative methodologies of manifestation. During this period, I encountered the seminars of Billy Carson, an expert in metaphysical science. Recognizing the potential value of his manifestation course, I promptly enrolled.

Known as an empirical researcher with profound wisdom, I took Billy Carson's work on manifestation seriously. His approach exemplifies the true spirit of scholarly inquiry; he presents his findings and advocates for critical thinking by urging his audience to independently verify and explore the subjects he discusses.

Carson delves into the intricate mechanics of manifestation in his seminars, and his insights offer a confluence of spirituality and pragmatism. His words serve as both a guide and a catalyst for those seeking to understand the fabric of reality and harness it to manifest their aspirations. This experience exemplified the essence of enlightened learning, and Carson's teachings have become invaluable in my journey of exploration and understanding.

The seminar was informative, and the water alchemy technique attracted me the most. Alchemy uses sacred science in manifestation. In this technique, with the knowledge that water retains memory, we send our thoughts right into the water to project our heart's desires. The memory of your manifestation lives in the water, and ingesting this water can attract and create what we wish for.

You may be wondering how to use this technique. Well, remember when I said that your thoughts are powerful? What if I told you your ideas are light waves that travel? When you speak into the water, the water stores this information. Let's begin the process:

Alchemy Water Manifestation Technique

Preparation

1. **Choose Your Intention:** Identify what negative feelings, beliefs, or thoughts you want to transform. Write them down on a sticky note emphasizing what you wish to release.
2. **Materials Needed:** Prepare two clean glasses, a bottle of water, and a peaceful space where you can focus without interruption.

Step 1: The Release Glass

1. **Pour Water:** Fill the first glass halfway with water and attach the sticky note with your negative thoughts to it.
2. **Focus and Release:** Sit comfortably, close your eyes, and take a few deep breaths. Focus on the negative feelings and visualize them transferring from you into the water. Speak to the water, articulation these thoughts, feelings, or fears.
3. **Acknowledge Transformation:** Reflect on the belief that water can transmute these feelings. Even if you don't literally believe water holds these emotions, appreciate the symbolic act of releasing them.

Step 2: The Resolve Glass

1. **Pour Negative into Positive:** Slowly pour the water from the first glass (Release Glass) into the second empty glass (Resolve Glass), focusing on the transmission from low to high vibrational thoughts.
2. **Focus on Resolve:** Concentrate on positive affirmations and resolutions. Speak them aloud or in your mind, aligning with gratitude, joy, love, or other uplifting emotions.
3. **Visualize transformation:** imagine the water absorbing your positive intentions, symbolizing the alchemical transformation from negative to positive.

Step 3: Absorption

1. **Drink the Water:** Slowly drink the water from the Resolve Glass, visualizing the positive vibrations being absorbed by your cells.
2. **Reflect and Ground:** Spend a few moments reflecting on the process and your intentions. You might feel a sense of release, empowerment, or clarity.
3. **Regular Practice:** If this practice resonates with you, consider incorporating it into your regular mindfulness or meditation routine.

I started using this technique to manifest the success of my new startup business—one that I had created with my childhood friend. I was sure that first-year sales would be no less than $400,000.

"I trust in the faith I have within myself to be successful. I believe I am the owner of a successful disaster reconstruction firm with a book of business. I walk in positive abundance. Wealth is all around me." I affirmed those four thoughts in my mind and remembered them every time I started to think about the future of my business. I did have thoughts of failure occasionally, but I focussed on remaining calm and peaceful, reaffirming those four thoughts repeatedly. This significantly helped me through a tough phase where I could have lost hope. And what do you know? In the spring of 2021, the Texas freeze hit, and my newly formed company crossed a whopping profit of more than $400k in a year.

My Journey Through Manifestation Techniques

I initiated a "book club" on January 13, 2022, centered around the captivating art of manifestation. In this vibrant group, we chose the book "369", which we all felt could help us manifest anything we wanted out of life. To ensure the group's success, I provided structure and depth to our exploration of manifestation. I segmented the process into four quarters, each focusing on a particular technique the group members embraced.

In the first quarter, we focused on transforming the book into a living journal, chronicling our daily thoughts and intentions related to manifestation. If you are familiar with the Law of Attraction, this section was akin to a masterclass, offering an in-depth, step-by-step guide on harnessing the law for potent manifestations.

As we transitioned into the second quarter, we delved into the enchanting realm of water alchemy, which I described in the previous section.

In the third quarter of our journey, we explored the mystical numerologies of the 333, 555, and 777 techniques. In the 555 technique, for example, we crafted mantras and wrote them with clarity and precision. Per individual preference, we repeated them consecutively, five times daily, and maintained this schedule for five days, weeks, or months. The 333 and 777 techniques followed similar paradigms with varying numerological patterns. The consensus favored the weekly plan, which struck a harmonious balance when manifesting results.

Among these, the 777 technique held a special place in my heart. The cadence of writing affirmations seven times in the morning, seven times in the afternoon, and seven times in the evening for seven continuous days resonated with me.

Finally, we focused on Tesla's 369 technique in the fourth quarter. This technique draws inspiration from Nikola Tesla's declaration of the numbers 3, 6, and 9 as supremely powerful in manifestation. The method involves writing down your intention three times in the morning, six times in the afternoon, and nine times in the evening.

The results were astounding for all of us. One of Latosha's manifestations centered on obtaining a pay raise. Using the 555 technique, Latosha received the desired promotion within five weeks of using the 555 manifestation method. Tareska's manifestation aimed to locate a musical director for her church. Tareska had a vacation excursion planned for May 30 of that year. She began utilizing the 333 strategy during the first week of May, and by the end of the third week, she had found the ideal candidate for the position.

Tareska's manifestation was that the new hire occurred before she went on vacation and satisfied all the requirements for the job, and that is precisely what she received. Our third member, Elisha, manifested an entire candle enterprise using water alchemy. Amazingly, the "Elise" candle business was birthed using the memory-storing capabilities of water.

Elisha had never run a business before, but by utilizing the power of manifestation, she could manifest this enterprise in the desired time frame. I have had great success manifesting as well. I manifested a specific sale price for the golf course property I used for an Airbnb business. In a significantly overvalued market, the house costs approximately $100,000 more than its actual worth.

I manifested a price at which I would earn exactly $30,000 over that sum. I utilized the 777 strategy, and approximately one month later, I sold the property for $130,000 in profit. It is imperative to recognize that the efficacy of these techniques is predicated on belief, positivity, and a peaceful state of mind. Combining these elements conjures a synergy that is instrumental in the manifestation process.

Keys to Successful Manifestation

The key to achievement is believing in what you manifest. The Law of Attraction is a law of the universe, and to use this law for yourself, you must first have clarity of thought. If your conscious and subconscious thoughts are not aligned, there will be imbalances and potentially unfulfilled results.

The best way to manifest an outcome is to focus on a specific course of action. Set your intention, make a strategy, embody it, and start putting energy into it as soon as possible. Pettiness and negative thoughts will not help you in life. It is crucial not to harbor fear either (this includes worries about yourself and others).

Keeping your frequency balanced is highly beneficial. Surround yourself with loving, kind, and inspiring people who can help you grow. Their joy can help you access your version of success. In addition, although anyone can become successful at manifesting, some circumstances can impact success. When manifesting, avoid any addictive and mind-altering drugs- like alcohol. It is essential to release any harmful distractions in your life.

Focus on letting go of any hang-ups that arise; release anger, don't start fights, heal fear, and release people who distract you from your life purpose. You must practice love and only love. Focus on yourself and the well-being of others (including Earth and other species).

Keep yourself on the most loving of paths, embrace yourself, and continue to awaken and light up your soul. This will aid you in connecting with the highest frequency of Quantum Entanglement. Everything you experience is vibration and frequency. Your feelings are your frequency. The more your feelings match up with attracting something you desire, the closer you'll achieve it.

When you open your heart toward something, it will reciprocate with positive abundance. Indeed, the power is in you to manifest and heal yourself. Stay peaceful. Keep your frequency of feelings balanced and positive. Manifest your purpose.

Manifestation is a powerful tool that allows us to shape our reality and achieve our goals. By adopting various techniques, maintaining a clear mind and positive outlook, and connecting within, we can transform our lives and open the doors for a loving world.

Instruction

Before you do anything else, you must be clear about your intentions and desires. Once you know them, the next step in the process would be to start visualizing the details of the desired outcome you'd like to see. You can do this by writing down your desires or creating a vision board to help you achieve your goals. Remember to focus on desires that help you and others, which aren't superficial.

The next thing you can do is figure out how that desire makes you feel. Does it make you feel joyful or perhaps loved? You will want to harness that emotion because it has a powerful connection to your desired result. Remember, emotion is e-motion, energy in motion.

If you can connect strong visuals with feelings, you are more likely to succeed. In addition to manifestation success, exploring emotions assists the individual to learn further exactly why they desire certain things and whether or not that thing is what resonates with their soul to manifest.

Once visualization and feeling are complete, it's time to make a formal plan. What barriers might be in your way of achieving your goals, and how can you overcome them? Planning should involve shifting your thoughts, focusing on the present you are creating, and visualizing the desired outcome.

Focus on the value of yourself and the situation. Tell yourself the highest truth and that you deserve joy, love, and healing. Visualize receiving the highest truth.

Everyone has skills, passions, and assets that can flow in beautiful ways to better yourself and the world. These aspects of you need to be opened, trusted, and allowed to flow.

The important thing about this planning stage is that you stick to it and don't waver; that way, your chances of success are much higher. Always practice trust, determination, and gratitude; before the process, during the process, and after.

How can you practice gratitude? Some people carry a gratitude journal to take notes regularly on all they feel grateful for, and this can include; the sun, people, birds, water, Mother Earth, food, joy, being alive, and even life lessons and challenging emotions. Some people may focus on saying and thinking positive affirmations in their daily lives (as a form of spreading and feeling gratitude). Anything that helps you feel gratitude is beneficial; there are countless ways to tap into this energy.

Being in the energy of appreciation helps bring more beautiful things to you to feel grateful for. Once you do this, you can appreciate how your life is blossoming. This will increase the flow of synchronicities you experience.

If the occasional limiting belief causes intrusive thoughts, you must recognize it and release it from your mind and trust the process. You are a limitless being in a limitless place.

Most importantly, do your best to tune into the hum of the universe by raising your vibration. This can be done by aligning your attitude, thoughts, and behavior with your goal. And if done correctly, these changes will be noticed by people around you through small shifts in things like your body language, frequency, and overall behavior.

Most likely, you will notice more signs from the universe through luminosity and synchronicities. Always acknowledge signs when noticed as this can increase the happening of them. Signs are a dialogue between an individual and the larger consciousness of existence, Source. (Ref 7)

Where to Find More Information: Further Resources

If you want to start practicing manifestation, you can find further information on the subject. There are plenty of resources available.

Even a simple Google search will provide numerous websites and forums with added details on the subject. Many of these resources house internal communities of practitioners, and advice will always be available when needed.

Besides guidance and advice, connecting with a community that encourages personal growth and manifestation is wonderful. One of the most notable of these groups would be *The Manifestation Community*. There are several manifestation Facebook pages where people worldwide interested in this spiritual practice come together to share stories and talk to each other. (Ref 8)

And if called, you can join my personal Manifestation Group, an experience designed to help committed individuals attain positive results. This group was created from my experiences as an accomplished Mindset Coach, QHHT practitioner, certified remote viewer, podcast host, and published author. Log on to www.JasonMedlock.com for more information.

The following resources are also recommended:

- ***The Power of Now* by Eckhart Tolle:** This transformative book explores the profound wisdom of living in the present moment and aligning with the power of consciousness.
- ***The Law of Attraction:** The Basics of the Teachings of Abraham* by Esther and Jerry Hicks: Discover the foundational principles of the Law of Attraction and gain practical guidance on manifesting your desires.
- **Billy Carson's seminars and books:** Immerse yourself in the workshops and writings of Billy Carson, a renowned teacher of metaphysical science. His work synthesizes empirical research and spiritual wisdom, offering valuable insights into manifestation.

Exercises

Let's explore some powerful exercises for your manifestation journey.

To begin, imagine it's a year from now and write in a journal about how the past year went for you. This is much more than fiction writing. It's a way of clearly imagining yourself in a position where all your dreams have come true, as well as the course of action that led you to get there.

If you prefer, you could also try keeping a manifestation list. This would be another journal entry, specifically a list of goals you want to achieve. What these goals entail will vary from person to person. This may be focused on finances, romance, life purpose, creation, and/or health. Whatever the focus is, put it on paper and, in doing so, give them a sense of concreteness.

If this doesn't resonate with you now, you can focus on rewiring your thoughts to be more positive overall, as this is key to getting the most out of manifestation. And the earlier you begin this process, the easier it will be moving forward.

And if you feel trouble releasing negative thoughts and feelings- even with the exercises already shared, then you can vocalize these struggles with other people that may be able to assist. You can also share your manifestation goals with others. Sharing your goals out loud may assist your determination to transform your desires into action.

If positive people know your goals, then they may be able to help motivate you and periodically check in on your progress. And if you take the full plunge into the world of manifestation, this could be a beneficial element in ensuring your success. (Ref 10)

Putting It into Practice: Embodying the Art of Manifestation

With everything you've learned in this book; remember that anything is possible with perseverance, love, intention, and trust.

Embrace the manifestation journey with dedication and openness, allowing these teachings to flow in your life. Remember, manifestation is an ongoing process that requires consistent action and focus.

As a recap, to deepen your practice and cultivate your manifestation skills, you may engage in the following exercises:

1. **Intentions journal:** Create a journal dedicated to recording your intentions. Regularly write down your goals and heart desires. Reflect on your progress and the alignment between your thoughts, feelings, and outcomes.
2. **Visualization ritual:** Set a specific time each day to engage in visualization exercises. Close your eyes, breathe deeply, and vividly imagine yourself living your desired reality. Engage all your senses to make the visualization experience more immersive.
3. **Affirmation practice:** Develop a daily affirmation routine. Choose affirmations that resonate with your goals and repeat them with trust and resonating feelings. Consider writing them down, carrying them with you, or recording them to listen to throughout the day. You may also repeat them as often as you feel called to do.
4. **Gratitude ritual:** Cultivate a gratitude practice by creating a gratitude journal. Each day, write down at least three things you are grateful for, including the manifestations and blessings that have already come into your life.
5. **Inspired action plan:** Take a moment to outline specific actions that align with your intentions. Break them down into manageable steps and commit to taking action consistently. Trust your intuition, and embrace opportunities as they arise. This action plan can be revised to fit your individual needs and may be consistently added to as you see fit.

Remember, these exercises are stepping stones on your manifestation journey. Tailor them to what resonates for you and your needs, and be open to exploring additional techniques that resonate as well. Embrace the profound wisdom of Source and embark on the path to manifesting a life of joyful harmonious love. With unwavering dedication, trust in your innate power, and the application of these principles, you will unlock the transformative potential that is within you. May your manifestations become a symphony of positive abundance, joy, and fulfillment.

Chapter 3

Hypnosis

Hypnosis is an ancient art form familiar to most but understood by few. Some see it as magic, while others see it as tapping into the subconscious mind (both are relevant as true magic is just the flow of energy manifested in the physical). How could hypnosis be of benefit in your life and the lives of others?

Unveiling the Essence of Hypnosis

Hypnosis is easily explainable. It involves entering into a trance-like state while awake, during which your imagination is heightened, your body is more relaxed, and your ability to be influenced is increased. A person will usually be placed in such a state by a hypnotist who can quickly help them transition to different brainwave states, but it does not necessarily have to be this way.

Have you ever found yourself driving to work in the morning and zoning out at some point, only becoming fully aware again once you arrive at your destination? That is technically a form of hypnosis you are experiencing. Moreover, if you do not drive, how about reading a book? Effectively, you are staring at a page and allowing it to put you into a trance while being able to picture the story.

Self-hypnosis is a form of this phenomenon. Most of us will engage in hypnotic activity to some degree every day without realizing it, and it is an excellent way to highlight precisely how easy it is to slip into an altered state of mind. But what about the suggestibility part? After all, that is what many people think of when they think of hypnosis, people being made to do or believe something untrue for a show.

It is true that if hypnotized, the heightened level of suggestibility you feel may make you think these things are perfectly normal. But a certified professional hypnotist's goal in a therapeutic setting is to help you heal and release negative limitations. The showmanship you might see on TV is present for entertainment, not healing. A beautiful aspect of hypnosis is that it allows you to become uninhibited for a brief time and tune out of society and all the worries it projects on you. (Ref 1)

How did this modality begin in the first place? Who was it that initially figured out such a process was possible? To find the answer, we must travel back to ancient times.

Connecting Ancient Wisdom with Modern Science: The Story of Hypnosis

As far back as the earliest civilizations, hypnosis was used in some form. Sure, these cultures may have yet to be able to verbalize what they were doing entirely. Still, they understood on a deeper level that tapping into the subconscious mind could be a powerful tool.

Often, hypnosis practices would be carried out by shamans. Moreover, their goals were to help people grow spiritually and/or heal more quickly from an injury through the power of suggestion. Whatever their purpose, the practice remained intertwined somewhere in the human mind after that, with some notable figures on the fringes of society, such as The Marquis de Puysegur, John Elliotson, and James Esdaile, exploring the idea of trance states centuries after.

It wouldn't be until the 18th century that scientific breakthroughs into hypnosis were made (that we know of). Furthermore, the only reason a breakthrough was made was the work of Franz Anton Mesmer, an Austrian physician who developed the theory of animal magnetism. This entailed the idea that an unseen universal fluid flowed through every living being and could be altered to induce trances and facilitate healing.

The concept of animal magnetism would eventually fade (for now). Still, the idea of trances being induced for a positive purpose got people such as Scottish surgeon James Braid to continue thinking about it when he coined the term *hypnosis* in the nineteenth century.

Braid knew Mesmer had been correct about the idea that focused attention could benefit society. So, with that in mind, he began doing further research into the subject, which would eventually create a legitimate field of study and lay the groundwork for what most scientific understanding of hypnosis is based on today.

This merging of the spiritual world and the scientific one helped hypnosis become more and more accepted to be treated as a natural phenomenon. This is precisely why researchers began to connect the dots between hypnosis and ancient Eastern practices such as meditation, mindfulness, and visualization as the decades continued.

Emile Coue, a French physiologist in the late 19th century, used this information to encourage the use of self-hypnosis to change a person's thought process and behavior. The results would help people embrace the person they felt called to become.

Then, not long after that, Sigmund Freud and Carl Jung, two of the godfathers of modern psychotherapy, began incorporating the ideas of hypnosis into their theories, with Freud and Jung believing that using such trance-like states, as well as the concept of visualization, to gain access to the unconscious mind could be very helpful in allowing the patient to heal quicker.

Jung even encouraged his patients to engage their active imagination as much as possible to help them achieve better health. As for Freud, his observations on hypnosis became a crucial part of psychoanalysis as he realized the importance of unconscious processes in people was more significant than anything else.

Even if hypnosis was being accepted in the scientific community (mainly for its medical purposes), there were still some worries from the public that it was a form of negative manipulation and could not necessarily be trusted. Those concerns led psychologists (such as Clark L. Hull) to attempt to demystify the whole process in the 1920s. How did they do this? Through research, Hull concluded it was nothing more than a normal part of human nature and something we all can engage into varying degrees.

That is where we are today, with hypnosis being so readily accepted as a legitimate practice that most of us do not even think twice about entering a trance-like state during a mindfulness session. Even the American Medical Association and British Medical Association both fully support the idea of therapeutic hypnosis. Nevertheless, despite all this progress, there are ongoing debates about how it should be used and when. Let us examine the scientific findings in more detail to explore this deeply.

From Trance to Treatment: Hypnosis Unveiled by Science

We have already discussed how today, hypnosis has become a legitimate field of study in the scientific world. What are some of the findings brought about by these studies?

While some scientists still are not sold on the idea that hypnosis is confirmed, most now see it as a phenomenon that does exist. Though according to the work of Marie-Elisabeth Faymonville and others (in 2006), they believe three components are required to be hypnotized appropriately.

First, they believe the subject must be the kind of individual who can fully absorb themselves in an imaginative experience. Furthermore, they must also be capable of dissociating and simultaneously playing the role of both actor and observer. Then, if both criteria are met, they must be suggestible in a way that will allow them to comply with hypnotic instructions. If all these aspects are present, all should be effective.

What has science discovered about what happens when we are in a trance? From the work of Faymonville, Alison Landolt, and Leonard

Milling (in 2011), we find that hypnosis can be a significant tool in helping people handle pain more effectively.

How does that work? Hypnosis can help decrease activity in the brain's anterior cingulate cortex, which links sensory stimuli to emotional and behavioral responses. Because of this, it can even allow women to switch off pain signals during childbirth (partially or entirely).

However, it is not just effective for the pain of childbirth. Further research from Tania Mahler in 2015 and Philip Shenefelt in 2017 has shown that the discomfort caused by gastrointestinal disorders such as IBS, Crohn's Disease, or skin disorders like Psoriasis can also be muted through hypnosis treatment.

In addition, hospital patients have recovered faster from anesthesia, depression, and stress through hypnosis. People have also been dramatically helped by using hypnotherapy in counseling. (Ref 3) One study by David Spiegel, MD, professor and associate chair of psychiatry and behavioral sciences at Stanford University, could even locate specific brain areas that were activated and altered. At the same time, patients were placed in trances (Ref 4).

Past Lives, Present Healing: Unearthing Insights Through Regression

Past Life Regression is typically used to treat current illnesses and imbalances (emotional, mental, spiritual, and physical) experienced in past lifetimes, but it can also be used for other reasons, such as awakening greater clarity about your current life purpose or healing trauma from suppressed memories in this current lifetime. Although reincarnation has been an accepted concept in the Eastern world for a millennium, it wasn't being studied in the West (by non-natives) for quite some time until explorers of the subconscious mind, such as Dolores Cannon, began using past life regression to relive past lives and record these experiences.

Dolores Cannon uncovered very astonishing details and insights into past life regression. It was around 1968 when Dolores Cannon and her husband used hypnosis to help a Navy wife heal her health problems. It shocked them when she went back in time to relive five other lives. The details of this incredible story are mentioned in her first book, *Five Lives Remembered*. If past lives interest you, I highly recommend reading this book.

I was intrigued by how the Cannons tapped into the higher mind to heal a patient. I wanted to experience it personally, so I did. I gained a greater understanding of our existence through my past life regressions. I learned about the incarnation process, how many guides we have, what foods I should consume while incarnated, what our mission here on earth is all about, and much more. Once again, my explorations into spiritual practices showed me that I'm never alone.

Hypnotherapy's Healing Power: Anxieties, Phobias, and Addictions Unveiled

Hypnotherapy is an effective method for healing anxiety. It has also proven helpful in enabling people to overcome debilitating phobias that could negatively affect their lives.

Research has shown that combining these two treatments (hypnosis and past life regression) has been effective at helping people heal a large range of imbalances, a few of which include: general anxiety disorder, fear of driving, depression, test anxiety, airplane phobias, elevator phobias, public speaking anxiety, anger management, sexual performance anxiety, and post-traumatic stress disorder. These modalities can be life-changing for people who suffer from such issues.

However, there's more. Aside from the ability to aid with pain management (mentioned earlier), in recent years, hypnotherapy has become a popular method of helping people quit smoking and/or lose weight.

For any smokers reading this, you may be aware of how difficult it can be to give up the habit, and anyone struggling with their weight will also be able to attest to just how hard it is to shed those extra pounds.

So, if something comes along that might make this process easier, why wouldn't it be taken advantage of?

Rather than focusing on getting someone to kick a smoking habit through the conscious mind (mental reason), hypnotherapy ventures into the brain and explores the psychological grip nicotine has over someone. This same method has also been effective when helping those suffering from alcoholism.

Alcoholism is a disease that targets the mind and makes someone believe they cannot function without a drink. Furthermore, while there are undoubtedly physiological factors involved in this addiction, the psychological aspect makes all the difference in decision-making, which is the main focus of hypnotherapy.

Is there evidence to support this claim that hypnosis effectively works to heal alcoholism? Yes, one piece of research by Irene Shestopal & Jørgen Bramness in 2019 showed that between two test groups they worked with over six weeks, there was a significant reduction in alcohol consumption in the test group treated with hypnosis. (Ref 3)

Journey into Self: Navigating Hypnosis for Transformation

It's time for the opportunity to try hypnosis for yourself. So, how is it done?

First, it is necessary for you to find a comfortable location where you feel safe and secure. Then once you have this, you will need to build some rapport between both parties so that there is a level of trust. This can be done by the hypnotist simply asking questions about what the person going under hopes to achieve and being open and honest with them about what the process can provide.

Once ready, the next step is hypnotic induction. This is focused on completely absorbing the patient's attention, so they focus only on the hypnotist alone, without any distractions. Doing correctly and gently should allow them to fall into a trance state. Then the client may be directed to gently close their eyes and roll their eyeballs upwards for a few seconds. Doing so will likely cause their eyes to start flickering as they fall into a state of REM, Rapid Eye Movement.

At this point, the client is not asleep. They are technically still conscious. Their brain activity should increase as they enter this different state of being. Once this state of being is achieved, the hypnotist can deepen the trance by keeping their cadence and rhythm calm and using key phrases such as, "You are now going deeper and deeper into this beautiful soothing relaxation" or "Every sound that you hear causes you to go deeper and deeper into this calm state of relaxation."

This part should be timely; however, the client must gently ease themselves in for the best results. That way, memories will flow easier when they reach the stage of using hypnotic imagery.

What is hypnotic imagery? It is the point in the session where the hypnotist focuses on awakening the client's imagination to begin journeying through their subconscious mind. This part is also known as the suggestion phase.

What is said to the client to help guide them depends on their specific ailments and needs. However, here is a broad example of phrases that might be used here to help guide them forward: "You are a beautifully confident person" or "Your confidence flows from within." This can aid the person to continue journeying. Next, the hypnotist may ask the client to visualize themselves achieving their ultimate goal, something they should now be open to.

Once complete, the hypnotist will focus on embedding positive and beneficial thoughts and suggestions so that when they wake up again, they will still feel healed and balanced emotions. If done correctly, once they have gently been brought back to consciousness, a seed of positive growth will continue to expand in their subconscious mind over the following days and weeks, eventually blossoming into something which makes it easier for them to live a fulfilled life. (Ref 6)

Of course, if resonating, you can also try self-hypnosis, which uses many of the same principles though the patient acts as both parties. That said, this can be more difficult to do, and so alternatively, you might feel more comfortable receiving a guided session.

Where You Can Find More Information

If you are looking for a hypnotist to help you with a specific problem, you can explore many sources online to find an accredited professional, such as the *General Hypnotherapy Register* (Ref 7) or the *Professional Standards Authority for Health and Social Care*. (Ref 8)

However, I suggest you do more research into the matter beforehand. There is a wealth of information about the effects of hypnotherapy on *The Mayo Clinic's website* (Ref 9) and via *The NHS* and *The Royal College of Physiatrists in the UK*. (Ref 10)

You can also contact the *National Hypnotherapy Society*, one of the leading communities in hypnosis and hypnotherapy worldwide. Through them, you can get your questions answered and receive assistance in finding an accredited hypnotherapist or even learning hypnotherapy.

Putting Hypnosis into Practice

You already have all the information you need for a beginner's understanding of hypnotism. Like any skill, it can take years to perfect if you want to practice it on yourself or others. However, this is something that, if you start today, you can expand upon.

That said, if you only feel called to be hypnotized by another person and feel the positive effects it can have, you do not have to worry about becoming an expert in the field, as there will be a professional who can guide you through the process. Again, you will need to open your mind to the possibilities of it and allow yourself to go with the flow. If you can do that, you become limitless in what you can achieve.

So, remember to trust in the process, be open mentally and relax, and release fear to discover all that is for you. Feel safe knowing that the person you are with is always there to help and protect you. Ultimately, hypnotherapists are there for you with loving intentions, so take advantage of that and have the best experience possible. Know that your spirit guides and higher self are there to assist you always as well.

Let us explore a few practices you can try at home if you feel called to do so. These are things you can do to attempt self-hypnosis. Effectivity can depend on the person, but it will give you some sense of how it works and feels.

Exercises

If you were hypnotized by someone else, you would first want to relax. Wear comfortable clothes; nothing that might be scratchy, tight, or heavy, and find yourself in a quiet room where you know you won't be disturbed. Afterward, silence everything around you (as possible). This means instructing anyone else in your vicinity to ensure they do not interrupt you, and turn off your phone.

It is recommended to sit or lay down comfortably. If you are sitting, it is important to sit somewhere that can support your back and will not leave you feeling cramped. Once that is complete, it is time to set an intention for the session.

For example, maybe you want to lower your stress levels or eat healthier to feel more energized. It could be anything. Zone in on the one primary focus of the session, and once you have that, find something simple within your line of sight to focus on.

If you do not have any apparent focal point, you could create one by putting a thumbtack on a wall in front of you or lighting a candle and focusing on the flame. Either way, keep your attention locked on this and breathe slowly and deeply.

Inhale through your nose, exhale through your mouth, and let your eyes rest on that one focal point in the room. Imagine that each time you exhale, your eyelids are getting heavier. Keep focussing on this until they feel too heavy to open.

Now you are almost there. The key at this point is to keep your eyes closed and focus on breathing, be mindful. You can always practice mindfulness exercises and meditation before a self-hypnosis session. If your thoughts are drifting, gently bring yourself back to your breath.

At this point, you can begin visualizing a mentally happy place where you will go, perhaps a beach or a field of flowers, somewhere relaxing to you. Got there? Now spend some time in that place, allowing your body to become heavy just as it does when you are about to fall asleep. You may repeat a mantra to yourself such as "I am calm" or "I am at peace" if you'd like.

Now, you may begin visualizing yourself achieving your goal. Let yourself see how happy you look and feel once you have achieved it. But, do more than just this. Affirm your goal to yourself while you watch. Tell yourself that you will achieve it and already achieved it; let your mind and body know this is what you deeply want.

After about five minutes or so have passed, prepare yourself to leave your trance state by imagining each inhaling breath drawing energy from the waking world around you. Each breath should leave your limbs feeling lighter at this point as you count down from ten. Say aloud, "When I reach one, I will open my eyes, energized and alert." (Ref 11)

Personal Past Life Regression Experiences

The sessions detailed below provide a glimpse of what one can discover during a past-life regression session. In these sessions, my spiritual teacher, Chloe Moers, goes into her heart space (located in the center of the heart chakra) to access feelings, visuals, and experiences of past lives that are ready to be revealed and shared. She and others can also use their essence to move through the chakras of another person. In the metaphysical world, it is known that you can access the past lives of another being by shifting your conscious awareness into the subject's chakra aura.

Exploring past lives can offer profound insights into the nature of our existence and the interconnectedness of our experiences. While accessing memories can be a challenging endeavor, delving into these memories intends to gain a greater remembrance and awareness of ourselves and access wisdom that can be applied to our present circumstances.

By sharing the transcript of these sessions, I intend to provide you with concepts and information that have expanded my perspective (and may expand yours), enabling you to cultivate a more profound and holistic understanding of the human experience. Remember, every person's journey is unique, and the lessons learned from past lives can contribute to personal growth, self-discovery, and a deeper connection with the world around us.

One thing to note is that our subconscious mind (and higher self) provide permission for what memories are accessible to the regressionist. As you will see, the information available is astounding.

A basic thing to note is that if the subconscious mind (and higher self) does not deem it essential to recall, it shall not be.

During this first reading, the regressionist and I established a safety connection. A regressionist requires finely tuned sensibility and intuition. During this time, I only participated in one meditative past-life regression session. My goal was to learn as much about my past life as possible so that I could better understand my incarnation experiences on Earth.

Here is an (unedited) portion of the introduction to that session:

Chloe: The way things work with past-life regression and the Akashic Records, in general, is that past lives are a part of the Akashic Records. [The Akashic records are the archives of all experiences, consciousnesses, information, and energies.] But time works differently than you might think. Time is not linear. Our perception of time, however, is generally linear, so, for instance, an event that happened last week we consider to be in the past and an event that is happening right now we believe to be in the present. But energy does not work that way. It's not limited to time and space or the way we think.

For instance, I can send energy healing to someone's future, and I can send this same energy to their past. I'm even able to connect and communicate with the subconscious mind of my younger self to help her. For instance, I can help her with an issue that she is struggling with or one that gives her confidence, and this will reflect in the current moment for me.

Energy, past-life regression, and the Akashic records are not based on linear time. You can also access what we would consider future lifetimes and future experiences. It's all just part of the energy of life. It is not necessarily the future, past, or present; it's all happening in its way, but we see it linearly.

So, with past-life regression, you can see the future. You can see everything, and what's interesting is that you can have multiple lifetimes at this moment, just in different ways. You can also see current lifetimes, but not necessarily in the physical body you're used to living in, which makes it very interesting. When someone else is guiding them, people typically experience regression in two different ways. One is hypnosis, and the other is meditation.

I am trained and certified as a past-life regression therapist using hypnosis and meditation, although I don't feel entirely comfortable with hypnosis for several reasons. One is that it is a very long process. There's a consultation, relaxation, entering hypnosis, coming out of it, and then grounding. The whole process can take about two hours. That's on average, and although some hypnotherapists perform it more quickly, the process is generally not less than an hour.

I have previously done regressions through hypnosis, but I feel much more comfortable leading people through meditation or quantum healing hypnosis. It is similar in many ways to hypnosis regression, but I feel it also allows the person to have more control in some ways. Not everyone does well or can be under hypnosis; perhaps it depends on how much you allow yourself to be hypnotized.

Interestingly, I have also had many individuals for both past life regression and age regression who are connecting to this life but just at a different age to bring up memories that they may not remember. Often, this is to heal habits, but it can also be about anything that comes naturally. I have been unable to go under hypnosis, which is interesting because some people can go under hypnosis while others cannot. Meditation has worked well, and I have taught people how to do it. I like that once you know the process, you can follow the meditation and do it yourself.

Here is an example of an unedited past life regression session I had with Chloe Moers:

Regression Session Part 1

Chloe: So, which method would you like to try today, Jason?

Jason: Mmmm, whatever you think is best.

Chloe: The other question I have is if you would prefer for me to first connect a few lifetimes for you and then guide you through the process, or do you want to be guided through the process to see what you can experience first and then for me to do a past life reading?

Jason: I prefer for you to connect first, see a few lifetimes, and then guide me through meditation to experience them myself.

Chloe: Okay. I will go into meditation to see some of your past lives and share some information about them, and then you can go into meditation. I will then view more experiences from those lifetimes I've already told you about or come across and consider other experiences. Sometimes, having information can spark a connection.

Jason: Okay, I'm good with that. I'm ready when you are.

Chloe: It will just take me a moment. I'll connect and see what information I receive. And so, the other thing before I connect with you: is there any specific thing that you would like to focus on? So, it could be natural gifts and abilities. It could be a career. It could be romance, family, a habit that you have, or a physical issue. It could be anything.

Jason: I would like to focus on natural gifts and abilities. I was shocked to learn that my soul's origin was from a Blue Planet that emitted light rays just like the sun, but they were blue. We also discovered in this lifetime that I was connected to creation energy.

Chloe: Okay, wonderful! I'll let you know what I receive.

So, I'm seeing information from your soul origin. I see your soul's origin on this blue planet; it's exceptionally blue. It's not the blue that we're used to seeing here. I'm not sure if you have the perception of being able to experience more shades or colors of blue or if this planet is just a lot more intense, but it does seem highly extreme. It is a blue that I've never seen before, and it's very bright, like the sun, but it consists of the clear light that the sun gives off. It is blue and exciting, and it seems like the origin is blue.

You have a lot of creational energy. You are connected to butterfly energy, but not in the traditional sense that we are used to. It does relate to metamorphosis, but its manifestation changed to exploration of life, understanding life, gaining perspective, and sharing this perspective.

It is connecting to a web of knowledge to expand upon this knowledge and connect people so that it will spark something within them so that they can continue this chain reaction of experience.

Now I am following this blue butterfly; it is very different from the ones we have here, although it has some similarities. It's more energetic, less dense, and less physical, but it still has some aspects like fluttering. It is very bright, almost unusually bright.

Does not have the same physical body, but the wings are the most similar. The power of belief is so immense. You can manifest the power of faith in the truth and in people.

It just switched to a different lifetime. This next lifetime is on Earth. You've had many lifetimes as well as many other things, but one of them that you did have was a polar bear. This is very important because you learned about scarcity, but not in the way that you may think. You had the availability of resources, but at the same time, you had moments in your life where there was much lacking despite these resources. You were able to live off the physical food that you would find, catch, kill, and eat because you needed to store energy.

Most scientists and modern people do not understand living off of energy. Not only are humans able to gather, accept, and absorb chronic energy, but other lives can also. Humans can use the light particles from the sun and other natural resources around us. You can gather this energy within yourself when you need some extra help.

One of the biggest reasons why many polar bears are currently starving, in addition to the lack of food, is because of humans. In some ways, humans as a collective unit have decided that the Arctic is dying and that the animals are dying with it. The indirect result of this belief is the starving polar bears because of the manifestation of this starvation.

This is not something that is understood by most scientists. They do not understand evolutionary cause and effect in the traditional sense. There was, of course, the actual starvation, but this was due to something else rather than just a lack of food or energy.

Beforehand, for a long time, polar bears were able to gather energy when they needed it, and it wasn't in the way that scientists think. You didn't necessarily pick a point through hibernation, extra fat, or the extra weight that they would keep on; it was way beyond that.

You learned scarcity, but you also learned how to gather your energy—not just your physical food but your energy food, your energy nutrients. This is something you will be able to transfer to others. This gift of living on light shows people what they can do and how powerful they are.

You were a healer who consecrated waterfalls to a different energy and a different beauty emitting from them. Waterfalls are a powerful energy source, and we can use them for so many things. They give back to others, to ecosystems, and to life.

The sound of a waterfall is also a potent frequency. You channel this energy throughout your being, and you can give nourishment and health to yourself and to animals on the planet.

You were this bridge of energy from the waterfall to the people, to the animals, to the land—the bridge of power and beauty—and it was essential. So, these are three lifetimes I gathered that came strong.

Jason: The polar bear's life is quite interesting. I am naturally drawn toward trying to live off the earth's energy. I once practiced prana living and being in tune with living off less, so this certainly resonates with me.

Chloe: Yeah, it was something I've never seen before. I've never asked the question about polar bears or different animals. Polar bears can absorb light particles and live off them in similar ways that humans can. Most humans are not living off prana—living fully; if a human does live off prana, it is like 1 to 5 percent, which is interesting.

Do you have any questions before getting started with the meditative portion of regression therapy?

Jason: Did I live in different periods? For instance, was I an Egyptian? Where was I during the time of the Anunnaki, when they occupied Atlantis?

Chloe: Atlantis... I feel this very strongly. You helped with the foundation of Atlantis, keeping it in balance. It required a precise balance to stay secure. You are very involved with this. Hence, you are very stable. You connected the grounding energy within it, balancing yin and yang. But not yin and yang because it's not the opposites balancing out; it's just neutral unconditional love balancing out.

You used some sort of physical, dense form of energy—not energy healing, but similar in some ways.

You were able to call upon and transfer it to different structures within Atlantis to keep them balanced and steady.

Many things within Atlantis were created and used by energy, not human labor or even a lot of physical resources. However, you made some things with material resources. So, they required a lot of energy maintenance to tune in and keep the right frequency to keep their structures alive and working.

You are very good at tuning these frequencies. I saw ancient Egypt, too, but there was a lot of pain there. It was painful, and you did not agree with a lot of the practices, so you fought back.

You did not want things to operate the way they currently do. It hurt your soul because you saw so much potential and so much beauty, but at the same time, you saw people causing harm to one another. You saw people using each other.

You saw that certain practices could be refined and done better, so you had a tough time. You understood the spiritual potential; you understood how certain advanced technologies' specific ideas were, but at the same time, you saw other places lacking, and it was hard for you to know that they were lacking. You have been in many different places in history. All of it has had its purpose.

Jason: I have had many dreams of being in some ancient city that used modern techniques. I could never stay in the moment long enough to get a clear picture of the entire experience. When it comes to tuning frequencies, I spent the first season of my podcast, *I'm Woke*, speaking about frequencies and vibration. It is a natural topic that fascinates me, and now that I understand this information, it just makes it that much clearer for me.

All the different practices I witness in my daily business mirror my experiences in ancient Egypt—constantly seeing how to fine-tune processes; understanding, for years, how to integrate your spiritual gifts to improve your everyday life dramatically; and seeing areas of the business marketplace in which we work that are lacking and having a remedy for them.

And I have one more question. Have I had any lifetimes outside of the Earth?

Chloe: Many There are more than I can count. We can move on if you want to. Move on to the next lifetime.

Jason: Are we using meditative regression therapy for this discovery phase?

Chloe: Yes. Okay, so if you would like, you can just lie down and relax to get yourself ready. I suggest playing a specific frequency in the background.

The Meditative Approach in Regression Therapy: Understanding the Process

My sessions typically go well, and I am left with a sense of understanding from what I learn and experience with my regression therapist. Before we continue my session transcript, let's go over how you can do this for yourself.

I use a music frequency to get into a deeper meditation state called "Extremely Deep Trance Meditation" by Greenred Productions; it is a powerful healing music track that is 7 hours and 38 minutes long. I typically listen to the entire track when I am meditating to understand a different lifetime, which can be found on YouTube.

There are a wide variety of other frequencies for meditation that can be found on a variety of streaming platforms. If you prefer, for instance, shamanic music and drums, you can use that, and then there are also specific singing tools. I think music is beneficial and can be very impactful for deep meditation. Set the volume that you are comfortable with so that it is not too loud, but you should still be able to hear it. If you find the sound annoying, you can switch to another sound or maintain an environment of silence.

After determining the music you will use, I suggest reading the guided meditation below out loud and then recording it for your session.

Close your eyes, relax, and bring your attention and focus to your breathing. You do not need to modify your breathing patterns; just be present and focus on inhaling and exhaling. Feel how your physical being is doing. Notice any emotions that you may be having at this time. Notice any physical sensations. Maybe you're cold, warm, or comfortable. Maybe you're experiencing a slight pain somewhere, or perhaps you can feel a tingling energy.

You may feel one strong emotion or a combination of emotions. You may feel tired. There could be a little stress or perhaps some peace. Just touch and be present with how you are experiencing yourself and life now. Be here and just breathe.

Know that you're loved, cared for, and supported and that you're a beautiful light being that's here to do so many positive things. Accept the love constantly surrounding you, allow yourself to relax your muscles, and just notice if there's anywhere in your body that feels like you're holding pressure.

Do light scans from your head slowly down your body until you reach your toes. Anywhere you feel the tension? Just breathe into that place. You can even say that you are breathing into areas that hold stress. Then, let go of this tension and just be present.

Accept the guidance constantly given by your higher self and your spirit guides. Accept where you are right now, the beauty of life, and life's challenges. Living in harmony and balance is meant to teach you precisely what you're supposed to know: you are where you should be, and everything falls into a beautiful place.

You are currently accepting light, unconditional love, and healing energy, and you are also uncovering your soul's mission and purpose. The spirit's mission and purpose are why you're here. You're receiving the knowledge intended to be accepted now, saving the energy meant to help you on this journey and experiencing the grounding light here on Mother Earth.

Let's begin:

Now you can inhale for 1, 2, 3, 4, 5... Hold it for 1,2,3,4,5.... Breathe out your mouth for 1, 2, 3, 5.... Inhale for 1,2,3,4,5.... Hold it for 1, 2, 3, 4, 5... Breathe out of your mouth. 1,2,3,4,5.... Inhale for 1,2,3,4,5.... Hold...1,2,3,4,5.... Exhale for 1, 2, 3, and 5. Inhale for 1,2,3,4,5.... Hold it for 1, 2, 3, 4, 5, and exhale for 1, 2, 3, 4, 5. Now allow your breathing to return to normal or slightly deeper than normal. Breathe in green, brown, earthy, healing, loving, and grounding energy with every inhale.

Also, see and imagine pink unconditional love energy with some blue cleansing water energy; breathe in these energy colors: earth, water, and unconditional love. This can be a visual process or just an intention. With every inhale, say silently, "I am breathing in earth energy for grounding, healing, and relaxation; pink energy for unconditional love; and blue energy for water, for cleansing," setting your purpose and intention.

When you set your intention in your mind, the energy of that intention naturally follows. This is the power of choice in action. Whatever you intend will naturally manifest, so be present and allow yourself to set these intentions. Know that with every exhale, you can just let go of any energy that no longer serves a purpose. Allow yourself to breathe just a little deeper than you usually would and just be present.

When you breathe in, hold for a little bit longer than you usually would; after you exhale, hold that exhale for a little bit longer than you usually would. Just be present, be here, and know you're loved and cared for. Know that all your past lifetimes have significance, your future lifetimes have value, and your present has meaning. Only some things will be understood perfectly now, but it is all being processed within your being.

Be present. Focus on your inhales. Relax, let go, and exhale. Just be here, accepting the relaxing energy and nourishing your body. Know that as you become more and more relaxed, you become more and more present in every moment. Un-tense yourself and go with the flow; just be here in the present moment, listening to my words, listening to your breath, listening to your soul and into your spirit, listening to your higher self, and being here to process each present moment passing by.

Now, as I continue to speak, you can allow yourself to feel more and more relaxed, not to the point of falling asleep but to the point where you can access yourself and your subconscious mind on a deeper level, connecting with your soul on a deeper and more intimate level. Just relax. I'm going to be counting down from 20. With each descending number, just feel more relaxed or present, more here, more welcoming of the energy given to you and surrounding you, and more accepting of past life experiences.

As I count down, you will fall into a deeper space and deeper trance, and if you'd like, you can walk down the stairs from your headspace to your heart space. Know that these stairs lead to the bottom, where there will be a door. This door will lead to a hallway with many entries you can access.

Behind each door is your past or future life. These lifetimes may feel like they're happening simultaneously with this current one. Behind each past life is a lesson to share, an experience to understand, and knowledge to embrace. Take your time as I count down from 20 to 1. Walk down the stairs and allow yourself to relax.

Twenty. The staircase may or may not be visible. It could manifest as a feeling; you may also experience colors. Allow many processes to calm the mind and your experiences.

Nineteen. Allow yourself to bring your attention down the stairs. Every lifetime you have experienced is there within your subconscious mind. They're within your chakras, and they're going down to about where your heart space is, maybe a little lower, to this hallway filled with doors that lead to your past lifetimes.

Eighteen. Relax your breathing so that it is measured and deep. Slowly allow yourself to continue, know you're loved and accepted, and understand that the energy surrounding you is powerful. You can use it to unlock so much more potential.

Seventeen. Accept love, accept the light, and accept where you are, continuing to move forward. Move forward in this process; take your time going down these stairs.

Sixteen. Allow these stairs to take you deeper and further within yourself. This space will allow you to access any past lifetime that resonates with you quickly; whether it's one or multiple, you'll know exactly what you need to know.

Fifteen. Allow yourself to breathe deeply and calmly, be present, and accept the love from the universe.

Fourteen. Continue slow, deep breaths, feeling the energy entering your lungs and releasing all that does not serve you, any tension that is not for your most outstanding and highest use.

Thirteen. Breathe in, be present, absorb all that is best for you, relax, and go down these stairs. Allow yourself to enter this hallway once you feel ready.

Twelve. This can be anything that resonates; you can align with flight or energy. You may feel like nothing or something, but know that the point is there; see that you are there.

Eleven. Deep, slow breaths. Breathing. Hold. Know that energy surrounds you.

Ten. You are receiving energy and relaxation. You are in your prime.

Nine. There are so many possibilities and doors within this hallway that you can enter and explore, and you can stay within your mind if you wish.

Eight. Say, "I am open to the potential that my past lifetimes must share with me. I'm open to receiving the information that benefits me from these lifetimes."

Seven. Be here and experience all your intuition; allow the feeling to guide you.

Six. You are here, you're untensed, you're more and more relaxed, you're receiving relaxation, you're receiving peace, and you're receiving knowledge and the divine wisdom presented to you.

Five. Soon, you can enter any of the rooms that resonate. Maybe you already have, or perhaps you haven't approached the rooms. Take time to choose what resonates with you and follow your intuition.

Four. Know that these rooms are responsive to your energy, open to knowledge, and welcoming to wisdom. You're receptive and here to continue.

Three. By exploring the present, you can open any room that resonates with you and stay within yourself.

Two. I am now receiving wisdom from this lifetime opening, and I'm exploring.

One. I'm now receiving details in any form. This could be visual, this could be heard, this could be felt, and this could even be smelled or tasted. Allow yourself to engage with any of the senses that resonate with you and accept this energy. Accept this, be present, and take your time with it.

In the next few minutes, I encourage you to explore, take your time, trust yourself, follow your intuition, and accept the energy surrounding you. Feel free to ask questions in this space. Know that you will naturally receive answers. You may talk within your mind or out loud in this space. You can ask questions, share thoughts, and experience feelings. You can clearly say this with your mind or out loud.

I invite you to join me on a profound journey of self-discovery and enlightenment. I have bared my soul and explored the depths of my past lives, guided by the transformative power of regression therapy.

After finishing this meditation, you will feel a profound sense of calm and connectedness within yourself. You've begun a personal voyage of self-discovery, diving into the depths of your soul and the wisdom of previous lives. The thoughts and energy gained through this meditation experience act as a guiding light, illuminating their route.

As we return to the regression session transcript, my words and experiences reappear. The power of regression therapy unfolds before us, revealing the tremendous interconnectivity of our existence and the transforming potential that every one of us possesses. Let's continue my adventure and explore the mysteries of prior incarnations with expectation and intrigue.

Allow the wisdom and peace gained from the meditation to enrich your examination of my experiences. We are ready to go deeper into the tapestry of my soul, revealing buried truths and embracing the transformational power of regression therapy with an open heart and responsive mind. Returning to the transcript, the sessions unfold, exposing us to tremendous insights, teachings, and connections. As you immerse yourself in my adventure, may we be encouraged to start on our voyages of self-discovery and progress, realizing that the keys to unlocking our highest potential reside inside the depths of our minds.

Let us prepare to enter the regression session transcript with fresh attention and eagerness, anxious to reveal the great truths that await us and to explore deeper into the vast horizons of the human experience.

Regression Session Part 2

Jason: I'm seeing a lot of faces pass by my eyes.

Chloe: How does that make you feel?

Jason: No feeling. I see a woman with long hair and a boy's face.

Chloe: You can ask questions of them. Think of it as almost talking to friends or close relatives. They will be able to share different insights with you; relax and allow yourself to see if the information is beneficial for you at this time. Energy can help you, influence your life, and impact the lives of others.

Jason: My head seems to feel like a lizard's head that has human characteristics.

Chloe: You may have been a friendly reptilian in a lifetime. There are kind and cheerful reptiles, and there are also negative ones. Pay attention to anything that you may feel or experience.

Jason: I can see clearly; it looks like I was giving birth on the back of a wagon.

Chloe: What did you experience when you saw this?

Jason: I am experiencing pain!

Chloe: Do you see this as more of an observer or a receiver observer?

Jason: I don't know if it's me right now. It was an image.

Jason: I see a lion looking off a cliff. Now I'm being taken by the lion, moving faster and faster. I just went through the lion's eye, and now I'm back in darkness.

Chloe: Is this scene still playing now?

Jason: Now I'm back traveling the cosmos.

Chloe: You're traveling through space to receive these different visions and experiences from different lifetimes. You can allow yourself to understand anything else that comes up and enable this cosmic journey to take you anywhere you are meant to go once you feel ready to complete it. For now, you can say the word *ready* aloud, and I will guide you back.

Jason: Everything is in a spiral. There are spirals everywhere.

Chloe: A lot of creation is within spiral energies and a lot of manifestation.

Now we will begin to count from one to ten. Allow yourself to become more and more pleasant. Go through the door. You can manifest an entry into the cosmos, or wherever you are in the heart space, the stairs will lead up to your headspace.

Open the door and go up the stairs, and know that as I'm counting from one to ten, as every number increases, you are becoming more and more of a physical body at this moment. You are moving more and more back into your headspace. **One** allows yourself to be uplifted. **Two**, coming back and feeling love for yourself. **Three**: noticing your surroundings. **Four**, see your presence currently, or maybe wiggle your fingers and your toes and just feel being present and absorbing this moment.

Five, coming up from your peaceful walk up the stairs. **Six, seven, eight, nine**—getting yourself back in this present moment, then allowing yourself to open your eyes whenever you feel ready, gently. **ten**, you are now back, and you may open your eyes when you are ready.

Jason: Have you ever experienced seeing a single eye during meditation? One big eye in the middle of space? Every time I would take flight while under guided meditation, I observed this large eye. As it opened, it took me to a different location. I kept seeing multiple faces of other people. There were so many images that I started to wonder if all these images connected to me somehow.

Chloe: You've had a lot of past lifetimes; it makes sense that most of these were either you or someone significant in that lifetime. It seems like this is a way that you're connecting and receiving, almost like the eyes of the portal that you're going through to experience different faces in different lifetimes.

There is something I want to share now. Before I do pretty much any session with anyone, whether it's energy healing, channeling, or past life regression, I typically go into a brief meditation for a few minutes and see if there's anything that I'm picking up before the session. I asked about your past lifetimes, and I saw a lion before we got on this call.

So, as soon as you said that you saw a lion and moved through the lion's eye, I was like, wow, that is fantastic because I saw a past life as a lion, and it's something I felt, and I don't know why. I shouldn't have mentioned it, and I guess this makes sense because if I had said it, then you would have known I was thinking this prematurely; maybe you would have thought, "Maybe I'm thinking of this because you mentioned lion" or something, but that's something that I saw strongly before we got on this call when I was checking in briefly.

Also, I want to say that it's incredible that you were connecting strongly; I was sending energy to you when you were in this space, but it's a way of connection; it's your method.

Jason: I've never, during meditation, seen an eye; it opened, and I zoomed in on a lion. It was so intense that I kept zooming so close that I literally went through the lion's pupil, and then there was darkness. This was certainly interesting; I was like, Whoa, OK! I could see the lion standing there, and the lion seemed to be overlooking a cliff, looking over the cliff or something like that. I also saw a little boy in one of my visions just lying there with a normal look on his face, and I saw a lady with a sharp nose.

Note: In this session, there were hundreds of images fluttering before my eyes. It seemed like a portal of some sort. Based on my research, what I was experiencing was just the interconnectedness of all the lifetimes—seeing, experiencing, the portal, adventure, and connectedness.

Chloe: There are so many ways to connect to past lifetimes; every time you feel your past life experiences, just remember they'll continue to evolve and change. What's unique to me, Jason, is that I haven't heard of the exact method of your connection.

Note: I explained to my regression therapist that most people start receiving visualization as a message. Many people sense their connections differently. I receive visuals with different pictures flashing in and out like a video playing. The more that I connect to Source, the more my other senses will be engaged; I will feel better able to experience the emotions of a lifetime, see more significant scenes of that past lifetime, and hear and ask questions. Also, with a strong connection, I am able to communicate with past lives directly.

There are past lives that I'm able to access and ask questions about, such as: "What struggled with you in this lifetime?" "What do I need to learn currently?" "Did I have a unique perspective on a particular issue or topic?" and "How can I experience another level of consciousness in this current lifetime?"

Jason: Interestingly, the more that you connect to expanded consciousness, the more that your psychic senses will continue to evolve. The third-eye chakra exercise that I've been doing forever has helped. The channeling sessions that I've been practicing are similar to connecting for past-life regression.

But this is the first time I can recall a pre-meditative session that took me places. When the eye opened, there was a boom and fast movement. Finally, when I stopped, the eye showed me things. This was the first time I've ever had this type of experience. It's an excellent way to connect, and now I'm sharing it with you.

Probably the most common method of connection I currently use for different methods, including past lives, is going into the heart space. Going through a portal was beyond the heart space, so now I'm seeing and experiencing the portal. Interestingly, it is a similar concept to connecting through the heart space, yet also different.

This method of connecting through the eye portal is something I will continue to develop and see how far it takes me. I'm receiving flashbacks of being in the middle of space. I could see the pupil, and when it opened, I was drawn closer inside the eye.

The strangest things were the wagon and the woman. I noticed her head hanging out the back of the wagon. She had long blonde hair; she was giving birth; she was being attended to; and she was in pain.

Chloe: I feel that was you in the wagon; what you were going through was identically connected. I had a feeling that that was an experience that you had. If you'd like, I can ask about its significance.

Jason: Okay, and I want you to also ask about the direction I'm headed. This current life I'm experiencing is a total shift from being a construction executive. Is this lifetime happening the correct way, or is it split? You know humans have a choice to go left or right, whichever path they choose. Let's say you choose left; this is probably the way this lifetime will end, but directly choosing the direction that you're currently on and that you have presently chosen is the most divinely positive path for you.

I never ask for specifics like, "Is this the correct path, or is there a more divine path?" I do, however, want to make sure that I am in total harmony with my subconscious mind. I have researched and found that your subconscious mind sometimes will not be too happy with you because you're not following the path before you, or you are not uplifting the consciousness of humanity, or whatever. Can you connect to my subconscious as well?

Chloe: I connect to higher selves, past lifetimes, and the subconscious mind.

Jason: I want to know from my subconscious mind that we are working together in harmony, and I want to make sure that I am not engaging in something that my subconscious mind does not want me to do. I want to make sure we are working together. I understand that the conscious mind and the human ego will try to answer every question for you and give you every reason to doubt or fear. However, I have come to understand that sometimes the subconscious mind feels like it's not loved. One reason would be that the human avatar is heading in a different direction than the subconscious wants it to.

Chloe: That birth that was happening in the wagon was you. This was traumatic for you to go through; it was very painful and traumatizing to your body and your emotions. You didn't get over the pain; a lot of women who give birth, in their minds, will forget about the pain of birth, or they will be able to move on from it.

This caused you trauma; it's emotionally hard for you and painful enough that you could use healing energy and some love towards that life, even if it's just sending some galactic energy. Just sending the intention that the distance energy is going to be received for that life would be very beneficial and healing; it was traumatic and very hard for your soul and even for your spirit. You are on the correct path, but at the same time, it's very important for you to truly believe in yourself. Believe in yourself in an excellent way to understand your potential more broadly and to know just how you're truly capable of absolutely anything without limits.

Understanding that you're beyond infinite is a fundamental concept to absorb for yourself. You are beyond that, so try not to constrict yourself to the way that others have already done things. You are meant to do something in a way that already resonates with you.

You are aware that within your subconscious mind and your soul, Jason, you do not follow other people's leads. Be your own leader. Others may inspire you, and that is perfectly fine and beneficial, but find your path and create something new, something that at times may leave you confused about exactly where it's headed. You may not feel exactly certain about taking the next step, but it's a new step that most others have not taken.

Jason, you are on the right path. Have confidence in your next step; we see you starting in the right direction, so expand your horizons of what is possible. Your subconscious mind wants you to know how limitless you are, how immense your energy and ability are, and not feel constricted by the way that society and other factors have been set up to operate because it does not need to work that way.

Understand your true potential in a more significant way, manifest bigger things, and follow bigger goals. Try not to follow them in the exact way that most people teach. You will find your own methods.

Jason: Can you ask my higher self again if I'm on the same page with my subconscious? I have been professionally trained in Scientific Remote

Viewing (SRV) and Associate Remote Viewing (ARV). I've successfully picked the future outcome of targets, sporting events, business transactions, stocks, and something as simple as picking which location I should take a vacation to and with whom. Is this something my subconscious is allowing me to experience during this lifetime?

Chloe: Yes, you are, but it's taking time for you to be fully aware of certain concepts and knowledge; that's fine because your subconscious mind is patient. I'll connect again for more information. Think of this remote viewing ability as almost the tip of the iceberg.

This is not the full potential of this gift called remote viewing. In general, it can give certain information very strongly to those who can see it, such as yourself, but it is almost like a piece of greater ability.

This is interesting because I just saw something; it's almost like being able to see. It's not necessarily about seeing, but I have a vision that you can travel with. You're able to travel. I just saw a vision of teleportation, which is interesting because it's not something that I see very often. They are saying not to worry about it because it's not about remote viewing; it's about connecting to the abilities you're born with and using them to their full potential.

So, what you're able to see, even something significant like knowing the winning lottery numbers or knowing you could use this gift in many ways is almost like the tip of your abilities. You're able to travel with this ability; you're able to change events and change energy. It's not about seeing. It's about what you're able to do with this portal consciousness connection.

Jason: In what direction do I need to be headed to harness this ability? I do not have fear.

Chloe: It's almost like not seeing in some way; for instance, you're able to see, and that's like the tip of what you're able to do, but it's not about that. It is about manifestation and changing lives. Changing things in a massive way. Physical travel is not like vision travel, but physical travel is a bunch of different things.

I don't think that they want you to get wrapped up in the concept of pure remote viewing, but rather to use this as a gateway to everything that you can achieve.

Jason: Okay, I think that's probably why they said don't worry about it, because it's important not to get too invested. They are saying, well, this is an extraordinary ability that I want to master, this specific ability, and become perfect at it and even have it as a profession. I see the bigger picture; this is the tip of what I'm able to do, and this is showing me all the potential. I must do things that no one else has done.

Chloe: It's very positive to win the lottery because you can use that money to help others and to do positive things with it, so money is not something negative. Money can do so many positive things; it just depends on how people decide to use it.

Chapter 4

The Third Eye Chakra and the Pineal Gland: Gateway to Expanded Consciousness

Ancient Indian spiritual traditions mention the third eye as a powerful inner eye, existing beneath the forehead.

According to Dr. Jill Ammon-Wexler, in new-age spirituality, the third eye symbolizes the state of enlightenment and the evocation of mental images with deep personal spiritual, and psychological meaning. The third eye is often associated with clairvoyance, ESP, visions, empathy, channeling, precognition, remote viewing, astral travel, and out-of-body experiences.

We've all heard the phrase "mind's eye" before—the imagination or picture one can form in their mind. In ancient religions, such as Buddhism or Hinduism, the third eye reportedly allowed people to view hidden inner realms that were otherwise invisible to their remaining senses.

Have you ever seen an Indian, Pakistani, or Bangladeshi person wearing a bindi, the jewel placed right in the center of the forehead between the eyes? That references the third eye—evidence of its importance in their cultures. And it wasn't just these groups that placed significance on the third eye; east in China, Taoism was simultaneously providing many of the same teachings.

Out-of-body experiences and precognition have been attributed to the third eye. Ancient stories tell of those who were able to reach a high state of enlightenment using their third eye, and those people would often become important figures in their community, usually acting as seers of some kind and helping to advise their people going forward.

What we have since come to describe as religious visions—a person communing with the gods and asking for guidance—may have simply been someone gaining access to the power of the third eye.

The Pineal Gland

Given the fact that two separate parts of the world with different people practicing different religions all arrived at the same conclusion that something is going on behind the forehead, this must have significance. Synchronicities are beyond coincidence.

People in the medical community agreed, with many doctors and researchers spending decades trying to see if there was anything in the brain that would directly relate to this awareness.

And that would eventually lead to the discovery of the pineal gland, a small endocrine gland that lies between the two hemispheres of the brain, directly underneath the forehead, deriving its name from its pine cone-like shape.

So, what does the pineal gland do? That's a bit more complicated to explain because although we have learned much about it in the years since its re-discovery in the early 20th century, there's still much about its function that remains a mystery to scientists.

What has already been confirmed is that the pineal gland produces melatonin in the brain, a hormone that allows us to regulate sleep patterns in accordance with both circadian and seasonal cycles.

The pineal gland also serves several other functions, such as helping us stabilize our mood and maintain good cardiovascular health through repeated serotonin bursts. But that's not all the pineal gland does; to some degree, it helps fight cancer, affects bone metabolism, and may combat the symptoms of aging, although the reasons for this are still not understood in the scientific community.

We have also learned that if the pineal gland is not working properly, it can lead to various unpleasant symptoms such as headaches, seizures, nausea, and damage to your memory, vision, and sense of direction.

Theories About the Pineal Gland

Philosopher René Descartes speculated that the pineal gland acts as the principal seat of the soul, which contains metaphysical qualities beyond our current understanding. He wasn't the only one who believed this. After quickly connecting the dots between the pineal gland and the third eye, many great thinkers of the era began to speculate if there wasn't more to be learned, especially when side views of the gland in the brain were later seen to be almost identical to the Eye of Horus from Egyptian and Mayan culture, suggesting that these cultures had some understanding of it too.

Some, such as C.W. Leadbeater, even thought that by carefully manipulating the pineal gland, a person could develop microscopic and telescopic vision, allowing them to look closer into the interior world with great clarity.

Stephen Phillips went as far as to assert that the third eye could observe things as small as *quarks* under the right conditions. As the years went on, however, according to his theories, the third eye would be used less and less, causing it to atrophy and eventually turn into the gland it now is. Since then, many other researchers have suggested that it still holds the ability to perform much of its original function, allowing people to gain access to beyond, under the right circumstances.

Take, for example, the work of Professor Nikolay Kobozev, who, in the early 1970s, concluded that tiny granule cells in the pineal gland may very well be responsible for controlling our thinking process. These very cells appear absent in people with specific learning difficulties and mental disorders, potentially making it more difficult for them to have the same level of coherent reasoning. So, with deeper access to these cells via greater stimulation of the pineal gland, it may be possible to tap into deeper levels of thought, turning the brain into something of a quantum computer.

You may see where we're going if you're a Marvel Comics fan, specifically Ant-Man and the quantum realm. It's been speculated that access to this quantum level of thinking could allow us to ultimately travel between dimensions in space and time, not necessarily physically (although this is unknown) but internally, through our minds.

There have even been cases of people having their pineal gland removed, which leaves them in a subsequent bordering state—they report finding themselves in two states simultaneously. In one of these instances, a patient even entered a bathroom but stopped short of halfway when walking toward the toilet. It appears they were bordering another reality, and something was blocking them from progressing further.

Implications

If what philosophers and scientists have hypothesized is true, the pineal gland may be the key to navigating these realities. If harnessed properly, the possibilities of what this could mean for humanity are endless. We may be able to jump between realities at will!

What would we find in these realities? What advances and innovations could we learn about? What wonderful experiences could we have? The possibilities are endless.

Different dimensions are real, not just a portrayal in science fiction; researchers have counted eleven dimensions of space and time already, far more than the four many humans were previously aware of. String theory has opened scientists' eyes to a whole new world of what's possible and real. So much so that the idea of a multiverse with infinite branching parallel universes is now mainstream knowledge. It's even believed that there may be a separate universe for every possible variation of every occurrence, whether it's something as small as forgetting to brush your teeth in the morning or something as large as getting into an accident.

The pineal gland could be our natural way of reaching these alternative planes. Our mind has already been shown to take us to other places—through our imagination and dreams, so what can our consciousnesses do? Maybe the ancient seers of the past communicated with other forces when they stimulated their third eye. Maybe they were traveling to another place or plane and gathering information to help their people.

The possibilities are endless! What if the ones these seers were speaking to weren't Gods, but instead, just us from another dimension or a different universe, one that might have been quite advanced with esoteric wisdom to offer? What if it was a universe where humans didn't exist and some other form of life had risen on Earth, one that was far more advanced than us and could help humans evolve?

We're not speaking of ancient aliens here. We're talking about trans-dimensional communication! And the thing is, that option is far more plausible given what we now know about the way the universe and the multiverse work.

DMT

While trans-dimensional communication is fascinating, let's take a peek into some scientific research for more information on the potential of the pineal gland. To begin, let us explore dimethyltryptamine (DMT).

DMT is a potent psychedelic that, when taken by humans, can cause vivid visions. Because of this, many cultures have used it throughout history for various spiritual reasons, such as communicating with the beyond and receiving wisdom.

What makes DMT even more interesting is that, with its reputation for opening the doors of perception and allowing for potential access to other dimensions of space and time, it shocked many scientists to discover that it is naturally created in the human body. Any guesses for which body part creates this? Yes! The pineal gland has been shown to produce DMT.

Someone who has trained their mind to create more DMT, such as a seer, could feel the full effects of what it has to offer. That's why many people have labeled DMT as the spirit molecule in recent years.
What could this mean for you, then? A school of thought suggests that taking DMT can open the door for your mind to access other planes of existence. It's even been suggested that the pineal gland helps us gain access to the spirit realm as our bodies die.

We've all heard of the light at the end of the tunnel that many people see as their lives flash before their eyes in their final moments. American psychiatrist Rick Strassman theorized in his book *DMT: The Spirit Molecule* that as a person approaches death, their pineal gland begins flooding their brain with more DMT, causing them to see visions of their life while also enabling them to open the door to that last moment before transition into the spirit world.

At some point, journeys between these planes may have been a regular occurrence. This may be the way people went to spiritual realms and communed with other beings in the past.

How can you fully activate your pineal gland? Well, there are various schools of thought on this, and the most popular techniques include third eye acupressure techniques, brain training, listening to binaural sounds, chakra stimulation, meditation, and the use of other psychedelic substances, which is believed by many to help trigger the flow of DMT faster.

LSD

In the 20th century, following the synthesis of LSD, many free thinkers such as Timothy Leary would begin to champion its use in helping people gain access to other realms, with him believing that this drug was mimicking what the pineal gland would do naturally. He thought, with enough training of the mind through repeated experimentation with LSD, the pineal gland could open greater, even if it had atrophied mainly over the centuries.

Ideas like this have made LSD very popular with creative types such as musicians, artists, and filmmakers over the years, which at one point gave rise to the idea that there is a connection between enhanced activity of the third eye and increased creativity.

Maybe the great artists throughout history who were once thought mad, like Vincent Van Gogh, Franz Kafka, or Brian Wilson, were not crazy at all. Maybe they were operating on a different plane, which made them seem that way to us. Perhaps they experienced increased levels of DMT activity in their brains, making them appear different from everyone else and opening the doors for them to create incredible things.

Mental Health Implications

Nicholas Giarmin and Daniel Freedman, two medical professionals who researched the topic in 1964, found that serotonin, one of the chemicals released by the pineal gland to regulate sleep patterns, was found in higher amounts in those who suffered from conditions like schizophrenia. While the average person has about 3.52 micrograms of serotonin in their system at any given time, researchers found that schizophrenic patients had as many as ten micrograms.

Could it then be that increased triggering of the third eye leads to a spiritual awakening? And, if true, would this be such a surprise? After all, seeing things typically beyond human reach could be too much for most minds. In the United States and Europe, schizophrenia is treated as a mental illness, but this isn't the case in many other parts of the world.

Cultural interpretations of schizophrenia range from the condition being seen as an otherworldly gift, to the person affected being haunted by spirits.[3] The degree to which schizophrenia is stigmatized or treated as an affliction directly correlates with the affected person's functioning and well-being, with those treated as "ill" having worse outcomes. One study of patients with schizophrenia found that American patients heard harsh or threatening voices when experiencing auditory hallucinations, whereas Indian and African patients experienced these voices as more benign and playful.[4]

There has also been some evidence to suggest that lack of stimulation of the third eye can lead to developmental disorders. A paper written by Tal Shomrat and Nil Nashir in 2019 indicates that in people diagnosed with autism, there is a relative lack of melatonin in their brains, a chemical produced by the pineal gland.

To be clear, I'm not suggesting that those on the autism spectrum are somehow lesser than anyone else. But it does provide some evidence that the pineal gland could trigger neurodivergence in the brain, an interesting idea to consider.

Fluoride Exposure

Health Impacts, and the Spiritual Significance of the Pineal Gland: A Comprehensive Review and Guide to Conscious Living

It can be a surprise to discover that synthetic fluoride is being put into public water supplies and other places, and people often don't see how significant this problem is. Fluoridation, like genetically modified organisms (GMOs) and tainted vaccines, is extremely harmful to human health.

How to Read the Fluoride Codes

There are two different kinds of fluoride to consider. Calcium fluoride is a naturally occurring compound in our groundwater and doesn't

---

[3] https://blog.shamanelizabeth.com/2015/07/04/schizophrenia-gift-or-illness/
[4] https://news.stanford.edu/2014/07/16/voices-culture-luhrmann-071614/

cause much harm, as it is present in small amounts. Overconsumption, however, can harm bones and teeth. The only beneficial aspect of calcium fluoride is that the calcium bound to the fluoride can treat fluoride poisoning. The calcium cancels out many of the harmful effects of fluoride in this naturally occurring substance.

Conversely, the fluoride added to our water sources and some drinks and foods are waste products from the nuclear, aluminum, and phosphate (fertilizer) industries. Fluorosilicate acid, sodium silicofluoride, and sodium fluoride are all fluorides that the EPA recognizes as toxic. Studies, like the "Comparative Toxicity of Fluorine Compounds," have shown that sodium fluoride, used as a pesticide and rat poison, is 85 times more dangerous than calcium fluoride.

What Sodium Fluoride Means for Your Health

Fluoride accumulates in the body, especially in bones, teeth, and the pineal gland in the brain, a recent discovery. Even though the American Dental Association still recommends fluoride to avoid tooth decay, long-term exposure can cause dental fluorosis- which can damage teeth.

Sodium fluoride is linked to other serious health problems, which are often not discussed and even intentionally hidden. Independent labs and well-known experts have linked the long-term use of sodium fluoride to the following health problems:

- Cancer
- Damage to DNA
- Thyroid disruption, which affects the entire endocrine system and can lead to weight gain and lack of energy
- Neurological effects; such as lower IQ, trouble concentrating, and Alzheimer's disease
- Pineal gland hardening
- Melatonin production issues; which decrease cancer resistance, speed up aging, and cause sleep disruption

Fluoride Inflow: What You Need to Know

Christopher Bryson, the author of *The Fluoride Deception* and an investigative writer, shared that the widespread use of sodium fluoride in water and food was a plan by industries to easily eliminate the toxic waste. In the 1940s, during the Manhattan Project, workers at nuclear plants and people in the area were told that fluoride was safe and suitable for tooth health.

In the 1950s, the influential public relations pioneer Edward Bernays pushed for adding fluoride to the water supply. The American Medical Association agreed that sodium fluoride could be added to water sources, and any studies or reports that said otherwise were discredited or ignored.

As a result, about two-thirds of the water in the US currently contains sodium fluoride. It is also present in various foods, including packaged orange juice, and even baby products. As a consumer, it's essential to read labels carefully and research the fluoridation policies in your city.

The Pineal Gland: An Amazing Body Part Affected by Fluoride

An expert, Jennifer Luke, did the first study of sodium fluoride's effect on the pineal gland at the end of the 1990s. She found that the pineal gland drew in more fluoride than any other body part. These results are significant, given how vital the pineal gland is to the endocrine system. The study put together the physiological problems linked to sodium fluoride and found a crucial player in the chain reaction that slowed endocrine function.

Minimizing Fluoride Exposure

Reverse osmosis is an excellent way to get rid of fluoride from tap water if you own your home and can afford to set up the system. If not, you could fill big jugs with water from reverse osmosis machines in health food shops or supermarkets. You can also purchase pure water from many stores.

It is believed that certain foods and supplements can aid in the decalcification and activation of the pineal gland, such as organic fruits and vegetables, raw cacao, chlorella, fruits high in antioxidants, spirulina, and iodine supplements. Always consult with your healthcare provider before starting any new supplements. Limit fluoride intake by filtering your water and avoiding fluoridated toothpaste and foods.[5]

Fluoride-calcified pineal glands can also be reactivated with easy lifestyle changes, such as spending more time in the sun, in nature, and meditating. This is important because the gland produces many enzymes and hormone functions, including melatonin.

Methods for Accessing the Third Eye

Now that information about safeguarding the pineal gland has been shared, let's explore ways to optimize and access its powers. In addition to the pineal gland's biological functions, the pineal gland is essential in spiritual activities. Yogi masters like Paramahansa Yogananda, who wrote *The Autobiography of a Yogi*, use it as a way to reach the inner or higher self.

Psychedelics

We've covered DMT as a potential tool to access the powers of the third eye. LSD is one potential chemical postulated to aid this process (although many people prefer natural products, such as Shrooms or Peyote). Shamans from South and Central America also connect with Ayahuasca, a mixture of leaves and stalks that activate higher levels of DMT, for spiritual initiation practices and healing of the mind and body. They call Ayahuasca, Mama Aya in many places. This approach to awareness should always be taken with the guidance of a knowledgeable guide or traditional healer, due to the potential risks. These substances can have significant psychological

---

[5] https://www.aquatechwatersystems.com/blog/the-truth-behind-ro-water-filters-and-microplastics/).

effects and are illegal in many countries. We are not encouraging or discouraging the use of psychedelic medicine; just sharing knowledge. These offerings are meant to help us connect the pineal gland in our physical world to elevated states of consciousness and other dimensions. Experimenting with DMT or other psychedelics as a trigger for the pineal gland is undoubtedly something to consider, but it isn't necessarily the safest or most recommended method. The following methods are other ways to help you access the full power of the pineal gland.

Meditation

You may have heard the third eye referred to as the third eye or sixth chakra. If you haven't, a Chakra is a term that loosely translates to 'wheel' and is a spiral of energy present in various body parts for different purposes. When connected and open, this also serves as our energy channel. The third-eye chakra is an opening for heightened awareness, intuition, visions, and psychic abilities. This chakra is a key focal point in the meditative process, which is vital to remember, as meditation can be a simple- yet powerful- way of gaining access to different realms of consciousness.

Meditation is one of the most effective ways to stimulate your third eye, and practicing meditation to open the third eye goes as far back as the concept itself. You may not fully activate your third eye on your first attempt, but with time and practice, this center shall awaken. Techniques can range from simple mindfulness practices to specific third-eye meditations, where you focus your attention on the area in the middle of your forehead or relax your focus into a candle flame. This focus can stimulate the pineal gland and help you become more in tune with your intuition.

Trataka (Gazing) Meditation

- Sit comfortably with your back straight. Place a candle at eye level in front of you, about an arm's length away.

- Gaze into the flame without blinking for as long as is comfortable. Attempt to relax into this.
- Close your eyes when you need to and focus on the after-image of the flame in the area of your third eye (middle of your forehead).
- Repeat this process for 10 to 15 minutes daily.

Breathing Exercises

Specific breathing techniques can stimulate your third eye and balance your energy channel.

Nadi Shodhana (Alternate Nostril Breathing)

- Sit comfortably with your back straight.
- Close your right nostril with your right thumb and inhale slowly through your left nostril.
- Now close your left nostril with your right ring finger, open your right nostril, and exhale slowly.
- Inhale through your right nostril, close it, and then exhale through your left nostril. This completes one cycle.
- Practice this for 5 to 10 cycles daily.

Sunlight

Some suggest that the early morning or late evening sun (beginning of sunrise or end of sunset) can stimulate the pineal gland. Always exercise caution when gazing at the sun to avoid damaging your eyes.

Sun Gazing

During the first or last half hour of sunlight, when the sun is the least intense, spend 10 to 15 minutes gazing gently towards it (never look directly at the sun during other hours to avoid damaging your eyes). IMPORTANT: Begin with 30 seconds - 1 minute daily and then slowly increase this to 10-15 minutes over time.

Sunlight Meditation

Consider sitting in the sun while you meditate. Californian zoologist W.F. Ganong has shown that the pineal gland responds to light. Sunlight can penetrate the bone in the forehead and cause this gland to extend, contract, and/or carry on in a continuous pulsing rhythm- depending on the level of light shining on it.

This knowledge helps us to understand many ancient religious traditions. When you step back and ponder their spiritual practices and sacred events, how many of them revolve around the sun and the stars, whether through solstices, equinoxes, or simply specific times of day for prayers?

Yes, it seems like ancient people may have known what we know now: the sun affects the third eye. So, try sitting in it while you're meditating and see where it leads you.

Yoga

Certain yoga poses are believed to stimulate the third eye; including child's pose, eagle pose, and downward-facing dog. Additionally, the practice of yoga (as a whole) can increase your bodily awareness and bring more attention to your internal states.

Balasana (Child's Pose)

- Start on your hands and knees.
- Sit back on your heels, then lean forward to rest your forehead on the ground.
- Stretch your arms out in front of you and relax in this position for about 5 to 10 minutes daily.

Sound Therapy

Certain frequencies and sounds may stimulate the pineal gland. The sound 'OM' is often associated with the third eye chakra.

Chanting "OM"

- Find a comfortable seated position. Take a few deep breaths to center yourself.
- On an exhale, begin chanting the sound "OM," drawing out the sound if your breath allows.
- Repeat this for a few minutes, focusing on the vibration of the sound.

Crystals

Placing crystals such as amethyst, selenite, and lapis lazuli on your forehead while lying down can help stimulate the third eye.

Amethyst Meditation

- Lie down comfortably and place an amethyst crystal on your forehead.
- Close your eyes and breathe deeply, focusing on any sensations you feel in the crystal.
- Stay in this position for about 10 to 15 minutes.

Sleep

Given that the pineal gland regulates melatonin, which controls our sleep cycle, ensuring you have a regular, healthy sleep pattern can help keep this gland functioning properly.

- Aim for 7 to 10 hours of quality sleep per night.
- Develop a bedtime routine and try to go to sleep and wake up at the same time daily.
- Keep your bedroom dark, cool, and quiet to promote better sleep.

Remember that any changes to your lifestyle, especially concerning diet and supplements, should be made in consultation with a healthcare provider. Everyone is unique, and it's important to figure out what methods resonate best for you. Each of these practices may take time to have noticeable effects. Be patient with yourself.

The Third Eye in the Animal Kingdom: Evidence and Implications

The pineal gland does a lot for us and is not exclusive to humans. Almost all vertebrate species have a pineal gland.

So, "Do other animals use their third eyes too?"

As humans can have a hard time understanding other species, they have found this to be a tricky question to answer, and while many, such as W.F. Ganong, have tried to come to some solid conclusions on the subject, we haven't quite reached that scientific level of knowledge yet. We do know that in Australia, there have been remains of animals found, since named the tuatara, which had a literal third eye buried deep within their skull. And upon dissection of this third eye, it was discovered that, while it was a non-functional organ, at one point it probably was active.

It appears we're not the only ones who can gain access to other realms. Perhaps at one time, our other species' neighbors could do the same thing. And if that's the case, who's to say they can't stimulate their pineal glands enough to do it again? Or that some even stimulate their pineal gland now?

And if it's true that some species of animals have started to lose their pineal glands through the process of evolution, what does that say about our future? Will we one day lose access to the third eye too? And if so, why would this be? Could it be because, through the synthesis of psychedelics, we no longer have any need for them? Alternatively, could it be nature simply deciding we've lost touch with it so much that it's effectively now useless to our development?

Perhaps the best thing to do, then, for the future of our species, is to use it ourselves actively. Whatever method you choose isn't important, so long as you do it with a pure loving intention. Maybe, you'll be able to experience things you never thought possible, things that could change the very concept of the world as we know it and push us forward into a golden age of wisdom and peaceful awareness.

My Journey to Personal Fulfillment: Awakening Inner Potential through Breathwork Meditation

Sitting in my living room, I began my second 20-minute meditation. After engaging in a focused breathwork session, I experienced an unusual sensation, almost like mild dizziness. I understood this to be my pineal gland responding to the breathwork technique I had just practiced.

My revered oracle mentor, Oracle Owen, had imparted this powerful technique to me. His teachings engaged me in using breathwork to stimulate my pineal gland gently. This creates a more profound meditative experience and sharpens my ability to visualize and manifest my desires. When I was around the 17th minute of the 20-minute meditation, I began to visualize and enhance my aspirations. One of the most significant was to sell my house for $380,000, with a target date of June 11, 2023.

As it turned out, the universe aligned with my intention sooner than anticipated. My house sold on May 30, 2023, for $367,000, slightly less than my initial target but still a successful manifestation. This personal example serves as a testament to the potential power of meditation for manifestation, demonstrating its capacity to provide a calm space for visualizing and bringing our deepest desires to life.

Let's delve into the transformative power of this technique.

The breathwork meditation technique I learned from Oracle Owen has been a profound tool in my life journey. It has unlocked a new level of consciousness within me, empowering me to reach deeper into my mind and spirit realms.

I have awakened enhanced mindfulness and clarity by stimulating my pineal gland through focused breathwork. This heightened awareness has opened new memory channels, enabling me to connect with my inner power more effectively.

Furthermore, consciously manifesting my aspirations has greatly enriched my life. This technique has helped me intentionally align my actions with a deeper purpose, leading to a more fulfilled existence. I can now steer my life towards positive abundance, not just in the material sense but also in terms of personal growth, happiness, love, and inner peace.

I've been guided toward my true purpose and built a happy and prosperous life by connecting with my higher-self. This tool of breathwork and meditation has not just been a pathway to increased consciousness but also a key to unlocking a life of joy and purpose.

How to Find More Information

As we journey deeper into inner realms, let's remember that learning is a continuous process. Should you wish to expand your knowledge about this topic further, consider these invaluable resources that can assist you in your exploration:

Embarking on a Meditation Journey

For a comprehensive understanding of mindfulness and meditation, look no further than the thought-provoking books Jon Kabat-Zinn and Matthieu Ricard authored. Their profound insights will guide you in effectively using meditation to stimulate the pineal gland. You may also find solace in the digital world. Apps like Headspace and Calm provide guided meditations for beginners and advanced practitioners.

Decoding Fluoride and Its Health Impact

The intricate connection between fluoride and our health remains a widely researched topic. The MENA Report has gathered much information on this matter, which is available on its official website. For an even deeper dive, peer-reviewed scientific journals like *Environmental Health Perspectives* and *The Journal of Epidemiology and Community*

Health publish groundbreaking studies that shed light on the impact of fluoride on our well-being.

Remember, each step you take in acquiring knowledge brings you closer to unlocking the full potential of your mind. Empower yourself with information, and the journey toward inner peace and heightened consciousness will become an enlightening experience. Happy exploring!

Unlocking the Secrets of the Pineal Gland: A Guide to Conscious Living and Manifestation

As you embark on this journey of exploring the pineal gland, unlocking its secrets, and manifesting your desires into reality, here's how you can continuously apply the insights learned so far:

1. **Embrace a Fluoride-Free Lifestyle:** Consider switching to fluoride-free toothpaste, investing in a reliable water filter/water source, and remaining vigilant about the fluoride content in your diet.
2. **Cultivate a Practice of Meditation and Breathwork:** Meditation and breathwork form the core of my recommended practices. Start gently, dedicating a few minutes each day to meditation, gradually increasing your practice as your comfort and proficiency grow. Use meditation apps, guided meditations, or enroll in a class—whatever works best for you. Incorporate the breathwork technique discussed earlier into your routine to stimulate your pineal gland.
3. **Harness the Power of Intention and Manifestation:** Visualize your deepest desires and intentions in your meditative state. Whether you're aspiring to heal your body or achieve a personal milestone, hold these images in your mind and imbue them with positivity, love, and focused intention.
4. **Persistence and Patience Are Your Allies:** Remember that this journey is a marathon, not a sprint.[6] Persistence and patience are

---
[6] https://www.obesityhelp.com/members/roxytrim/blog/2015/04/13/post/roxytrim's Blog. https://www.obesityhelp.com/members/roxytrim/blog/2015/04/13/post/don't expect immediate results.

your loyal companions on this path. Keep showing up for yourself, consistently maintain your practices, and trust the process.

You'll stimulate your pineal gland and be guided toward a mindful, conscious, and fulfilling life through meditation, mindfulness, practice, visualization, and love. Your journey begins here as you turn the pages of this book and extends far beyond into the realms of your existence.

Chapter 5

Deciphering the Psychedelic Experience: A Deep Dive into the Realm of Psychedelic Substances

As I continued my search for ways to awaken, I began studying psychedelics. I wondered; *can psilocybin mushrooms profoundly affect how we see our lives? Do they serve a spiritual purpose?* As you might be aware, psychedelics have been very controversial over the years and a point of contention in the U.S. Currently, psychedelic mushrooms are illegal in some states. So, why is this such a taboo subject?

Suppose we remove all the social hysteria and scare tactics around these substances. In that case, we can see that while there can be risks involved in using them, especially when done under the wrong conditions, there can also be many positive benefits. I will discuss the benefits briefly, but for now, let's break down what psychedelic substances are.

In short, these substances have hallucinogenic qualities, making them different from stimulants such as cocaine and caffeine, depressants like alcohol, or painkillers- which range from aspirin to opium. Whether legal or not, all these substances somehow alter your mind. Psychedelics, however, specifically target your sensory perceptions and thought processes, which can lead to vivid hallucinations, an altered perception of time, and a heightened sense of awareness.

Among the most popular of these substances are LSD, DMT, mescaline, and psilocybin, each of which can cause users to go on trips by activating the serotonin 2A receptor. This means that when the drug compounds reach your receptors, they will bind with them, modulating the activity of critical circuits in the brain involved with sensory perception and cognition by reducing default mode network activity and increasing connectivity between regions in the brain.

In summary, when specific compounds reach the brain, it affects the brain's receptors and causes the previously mentioned effects to occur. During these trips, as the user ventures into their subconscious, they can often find themselves undergoing life-changing experiences, seeing and hearing things rooted deep inside their mind. As such, this can awaken essential truths within the individual and lead them to life-changing realizations.

Psychedelic Origins: Unveiling the Source of Altered States

Where do these substances come from? Well, that all depends on which one you're asking about. In the case of LSD, for example, a substance more commonly known by its street name, *acid*, was first chemically synthesized in a laboratory during the 1960s. As for DMT, mescaline, and psilocybin; they have far more natural origins, with DMT coming from a plant found in South America, mescaline being a naturally occurring substance that's drawn from certain types of cacti, and psilocybin (magic mushrooms), being found throughout Earth.

For those who use these substances, the fact that they grow naturally throughout the world will always be part of their argument for legalization. After all, if they grow naturally all over the earth, why would the government have any authority to ban them?

In addition to this, the use of psychedelic substances among early cultures was commonplace. Evidence shows that Indigenous American cultures have used mescaline for six millennia. For spiritual reasons, in many tribes, the belief was that the person who ingested this communicated with gods during the process. Historically, various tribes throughout Africa have also taken mushrooms for similar purposes, often as a big part of their religious experience.

For anyone who has tried hallucinogens, it's easy to see why they are often associated with religious practices. The experience of ingesting these substances can often be so intense and vivid that analytical explanations fall short to explain. Although illegal in the U.S. and much of Europe, they're still used legally within many cultures.

And why is this? As mentioned before, there are controversies involved in using psychedelics, which has led to more conservative circles being far more reluctant to accept them. That's why, since the late 1960s, LSD and psilocybin have been classified as Schedule 1 drugs in the United States, with many other nations following suit with this assessment around the same time.

Of course, there has long been speculation about the real reason behind such decisions. Cannabis, the most widely used recreational drug at the time, endured years of government persecution before becoming illegal.

I'm not going to discuss the pros and cons of cannabis, but what I will say is that, at the time, the substance was correlated with African Americans and Mexicans, with the former group making the drug synonymous with jazz music and the latter group associated with the derogatory name the substance was given around this time, *marijuana*.

So, with that in mind, reading between the lines a little, it could indeed be argued that there was a racial aspect to the demonization and criminalization of the drug. On top of this, notorious media mogul William Randolph Hearst had his part to play in the situation, seeing the potential for hemp products to cut into his earnings. He allegedly used his political power to push for the criminalization of cannabis at this point.

And once opened, it was tough to close. From that point on, it became effortless to get laws passed against any substance that was being demonized, and this is what ultimately led to the passing of the Staggers-Dodd Bill of 1968- which declared that all usage of psychedelics would be deemed illegal within the United States. Three years later, the United Nations signed a treaty known as the Convention on Psychotropic Substances of 1971 to slow the spread of psychedelics worldwide.

And what a shame this was because, from that point on, research being done into the potential positive uses of the substances in question ground to a halt, with no one able to get funding for such experiments anymore, given their boogeyman status amongst the scientific community. But what makes this more hypocritical is that the U.S. President at the time, Richard Nixon, was using the war on drugs to build support amongst his base while his government was still carrying out highly secretive experiments as part of the MK-Ultra program.

Reviving Psychedelic Research: A New Era for Mental Health

If you want a more detailed explanation of what happened there, research Project MK-Ultra on Google. The secret experimentations aimed to see if psychedelics worked to open gateways to different planes of existence. And while, in the end, the U.S. could not find any solid evidence of this being the case, there was still a solid base of people who stood by the benefits of psychedelic use, with the most notable of these probably being Timothy Leary.

As one of his era's most prominent clinical psychologists, Leary would be an early advocate for psychedelics, particularly LSD. He even went on a nationwide tour during the early 1960s, speaking on college campuses everywhere he could preach about the benefits of "turning on, tuning in, and dropping out."

But while this put Leary at odds with Nixon for the rest of the decade, leading to his arrest on 36 separate occasions, this didn't cause him to give up. Leary believed that if proper research could be done into psychedelics, evidence would show many positive psychological benefits associated with their use. He even suggested that they could be used to treat mental health issues, such as depression and anxiety. And, as we'll explore later, while he never got a chance to prove this during his lifetime scientifically, history appears to have shown he was correct with this line of thinking.

This meant little to most governing bodies, as during the 1980s, with the rise in right-wing politics spearheaded by Ronald Reagan in the U.S. and Margaret Thatcher in the U.K., psychedelics became even more demonized. This would lead to even stricter laws against them being instituted, such as the Comprehensive Crime Control Act of 1984.

As this happened, the total hypocrisy of the war on drugs would continue to show itself. While alcoholism and cancer rates from tobacco use continued to skyrocket, the FDA would approve a newly synthesized drug named Ketamine for use as a sedative. Despite the drug's advantageous medicinal properties, it would also become illegal by the 1990s, when it had gained popularity as a party drug among young people.

Fortunately, in recent years, there has been a fightback over banning psychedelics. Finally, after 50 years of psychedelics being outlawed in terms of medical research, Johns Hopkins Medicine was awarded funding to investigate the potential positive psychiatric effects of using psilocybin in 2021. This seems to have helped open the floodgates somewhat, as now further research is being done into the likes of LSD and other psychedelics, with many scientists now believing that this could lead to a revolution in the way we treat mental health problems.

Take, for example, Ketamine, the previously mentioned popular party drug and horse tranquilizer that exhibits psychoactive effects when used by humans. When tested on people with various mental health conditions, the data suggested that it could positively affect erratic brain patterns and thought processes. Incredibly, it appeared to be able to do this within a matter of hours, whereas, by comparison, our current mainstream treatments for depression can take weeks to have an effect. So, with that said, we may very well be on the frontier of a new era for medicine, and it may be, in many ways, down to the positive benefits of psychedelic substances.

With this being the case, there are some potential risks when taking these substances under the wrong circumstances. Things such as the environment a person is in at the time and their mental state, can significantly impact the outcome.

So, if you are ever going to try psychedelics, whether it be for medical or spiritual purposes, you should make sure that you're in an environment where you feel comfortable, with trusted people around you, all while ensuring you're in a balanced state of mind before you begin.

My Psychedelic Journey
My mission is to explore and share various levels of consciousness, and mushrooms were next on my list. I wanted to explore the human ego and communicate with my higher self. I was introduced to the Albino Mushroom by a colleague of mine. At first, I was hesitant because I didn't know what to expect when purchasing it. I looked at the powdery substance with a mixture of wonder and disbelief. I guess the doors of perception can arrive in a variety of forms.

For my first attempt, I followed the prescribed process: 1.5 grams of the Albino strand, a glass of water or juice, and I also had my monitor present for when I was sleeping. After taking my first dose, I relaxed because I knew this trip could last four to six hours. After 30 to 40 minutes, I started to feel the effects, and it was a feeling that I had never experienced before.

As I lay there with my eyes closed and half asleep, I started to experience parts of my body tingling. The sensation was similar to what I experienced when I tried astral travel: your body starts to tingle in a specific area, and then the tingling sensation engulfs your entire body.

So, I'm lying in bed, and I begin to experience my astral body detaching from my physical body.

Once fully detached, I found myself observing conversations I had had with colleagues of mine over the previous weeks. What a unique experience! The colors were so vivid that it was like watching not a 4K ultra-HD movie but a 100K super-ultra-HD movie. I saw my ego up close and how it affected the people who love me the most. I asked, "Why is this guy treating everyone he meets so badly?" I would zoom in and observe myself. I had a front-row seat, watching the other person and seeing how they felt after conversing with me.

Once I woke and things returned to normal, I began extensively researching all mind-altering/mind-awakening substances. I needed answers. For one thing, I knew I would eventually share my findings in this book, and I needed to be adequately informed.

Guidance and Safety: Navigating Psychedelic Experiences

Being with people you trust is particularly crucial because there have been incidents in the past of people getting high, and without someone to guide them through the process, they have ended up hurting themselves. Luckily, however, even if you don't have a friend who can help you through this experience, many cities throughout Europe, the U.S., and the rest of the world have psychedelic societies that can help you. There are even apps nowadays to help you manage your trip.

Of course, given the legal status of these substances in many places, I am not recommending that you try them, but the information is certainly out there if you search for it. And if you're undergoing a trip for medical or spiritual purposes, the whole event can take up to 12 hours from start to finish (depending on the specific substance and your body). At this point, most experienced users will suggest you begin with a small dose, letting your brain see what it is like before delving any further. I started with 1.5 grams of psilocybin; this is typically a safe dosage, and I had unforgettable experiences.

If you enjoy the experience, consider increasing the dosage during subsequent trips, hopefully feeling more positive effects each time. I plan to take 2 grams for my next trip, a slight increase that should allow me to experience even more than I did on my first trip. My experience and what I've read tell me that your first trip should relieve any psychological issues you may be undergoing. You'll also probably find yourself diving deep into the recesses of your psyche while you're at it.

If you start experiencing a bad trip, you can expect, in the short term at least, to feel symptoms such as an increased heart rate, nausea, difficulty sleeping, and panic. This can be very confusing and, under certain circumstances, very scary. So, with that in mind, know that you should always have someone you trust there to help guide you if needed- even if this isn't your first time using it. I take these safety precautions seriously, so I used a monitor for my first planned trip to ensure nothing drastic happened while sleeping.

At the same time, of course, you shouldn't let these potential risks scare you away from the idea of trying psychedelics; most people find themselves having a positive experience, which is often transcendent. We cannot allow fear to dictate our lives. Some people have even believed they spoke to God during these trips, while creative artistic masterworks have inspired others. Some people have had far less dramatic but also very positive trips. Rather than communing with a higher power or creating a masterpiece, they've unlocked a new perspective on life and their place within existence.

The Two-Sided Coin of Psychedelics: A Balanced Perspective

The intentional use of psychedelics has led many to reassess their lives and re-evaluate what they want out of life, prompting them to make the necessary changes soon after the experience. From one perspective, like how therapy works, psychedelic trips aren't telling you anything about yourself that you don't already know, they're just providing you with an access point for understanding yourself better. For this reason, it's no surprise that even some therapists have turned to psychedelics, in microdoses, in one-on-one sessions to help people work through their issues more efficiently. A recent study showed that up to 65% of those tested experienced positive effects from such microdosing therapy.

This goes beyond helping those with mental imbalances. Research has even suggested that, among a % of test subjects with terminal illnesses like cancer, up to 80% of them felt these substances positively affected their state of mind during their final days. On top of that, those with non-terminal illnesses reported that the positive psychological effects of microdosing psychedelics helped them return to health. This should come as no surprise, as many doctors believe that a positive mindset is one of the best tools a person can have in healing a severe illness because a positive mentality helps keep the body strong when it's under extreme stress.

The potential benefits of microdosing extend even further. Recent research has suggested that those who have PTSD (post-traumatic stress disorder), eating disorders, or even drug addiction can benefit from micro-dosing, with psilocybin seeming to prove particularly effective in helping people quit smoking.

All medicines can, depending on how they are used, serve both positive and negative functions, and when it comes to psychedelics, it appears that the world is finally starting to wake up to this idea. That's why there has been an increased push for the legalization of these substances in many places recently. Take Detroit, Michigan, a city that has seen itself as home to a growing movement for decriminalizing psychedelics. And while this wouldn't make them legal as such, it would classify them as a low priority for the police to investigate, allowing police to spend their time dealing with critical crimes.

But aside from the obvious benefits of more efficient police work and increased medical research being performed, advocates for decriminalization also argue that decriminalization would allow for much of the stigma to be taken away from such substances, leading to far fewer unnecessary prison sentences, which only serve to clog up the judiciary system and cost taxpayers billions every year- not to mention being immoral.

On top of this, in September of 2021, Michigan State Senator Jeff Irwin introduced Senate Bill SB631, which aims to decriminalize the manufacture, possession, delivery, and use of hallucinogenic plants state-wide. This bill has even found support among high-ranking government officials, such as New York Congresswoman Alexandria Ocasio-Cortez, who has a long history of being more forward-thinking in her beliefs. Will this lead to any significant changes soon? It's certainly a possibility. But that doesn't mean it will be a free-for-all where everyone suddenly has unlimited access to these substances.

It's well documented that these substances can have adverse side effects in some cases, including paranoia and even psychosis. On top of this, while studies show that most psychedelics are not considered addictive, some, such as LSD, can be. And if used long-term, they can also trigger irreparable side effects, such as hallucinogen-persisting perception disorder (HPPD) or, in some more extreme cases, even schizophrenia.

Again, this is not to scare you off using such substances but to give you more information; ultimately, the benefits outweigh the risks. Yes, there are risks to using any substance, but if we could all be better educated on them, we can make more informed decisions about how we interact with them. So, I'd suggest that instead of governing bodies providing you with all the necessary information, go out and research the subject. And after that, go from there if it feels right for you.

And if you do decide to try a psychedelic substance or micro-dosing, always take care, and if you are in a more sensitive state of mind, be wary of what you're taking. The key is loading yourself with all the necessary information before any potential trip. If you do that, then you're far more likely to have a good experience. And for those still interested in trying it out, I'll leave you with one more example of what you may experience when undergoing a trip, which can show both the good and challenging sides of the experience: the concept of ego death.

Some of you will have heard of this before, but for those who haven't, it's the idea of reaching a point during a trip where you realize that you're not the things you have identified yourself as. It's a complex concept to understand, unless you've already experienced it. Those who have gone through it have often reported feeling a profound sense of peace and connectedness to the universe, as the walls they'd built up for themselves throughout their lifetime crumbled and their egos were balanced.

On the other hand, however, some may find this to be a far more terrifying experience as for some it can lead to high levels of distress and confusion. Either way, it's often seen as a life-changing experience and the pinnacle of what some users seek to achieve—an actual moment of spiritual awakening.

Yes, psychedelics are a two-sided coin. While the negative associations have been well documented over the years, the positive side effects often outweigh this with true spiritual development, better treatment for long-term illnesses, and a better understanding of the world around us. So, with all the information in front of you, the decision is yours.

And with that, I hope you found this interesting and valuable. Remember, you are a co-creator, and you are here to learn. So, open your mind to the limitless possibilities this world has to offer.

Chapter 6

Experiencing the Modality of Remote Viewing

Remote viewing, also known as RV or SRV (scientific remote viewing), is a phenomenon where a person uses the mind to perceive information about a remote location, person, or event that is not accessible through their physical senses or prior knowledge. It is often considered a form of extrasensory perception or psychic ability.

The Controversial Journey of Remote Viewing: Past, Present, and Future

I can attest to the power of remote viewing. Still, opinions about whether remote viewing is possible are split, with many in the scientific community labeling it a pseudoscience. At the same time, those who know of its powerful potential continue striving to find scientific proof of its existence. This has led to a few experiments being carried out over the years, primarily by the US Government during the era of MK-Ultra after WWII.

Of course, RV goes far further than this, as far back as the mid-nineteenth century. That was when many scientists first grew interested in the idea of telaesthesia and traveling clairvoyance, two things that had, up until then, been relegated to the realm of the occult. But feeling like there was something more to those ideas, early researchers like Alfred Russel Wallace, Rufus Osgood Mason, William Crookes, and Michael Faraday would each spend a lot of time and resources carrying out their experiments trying to prove if such a concept could be achieved.

There has been more experimentation since the 20th century when the US government began studying and experimenting with psychic phenomena as part of its Cold War efforts. In the 1970s, the US military initiated a top-secret program called the Stargate Project, which aimed to investigate the potential military applications of psychic abilities such as remote viewing.

The Stargate Project employed military personnel with psychic abilities and trained them in remote viewing techniques. They used their abilities to gather information on various targets, such as military bases and weapons facilities, that were difficult or impossible to access through traditional means. The program continued until 1995, when it was declassified and disbanded due to a lack of scientific evidence and political scrutiny.

Scientific Exploration of Remote Viewing: Targ, Puthoff, and Swann

In the 1970s, researchers Russell Targ and Harold Puthoff conducted a series of experiments on remote viewing at Stanford Research Institute. They trained a psychic named Ingo Swann to view remote locations and objects, and their results got published in scientific journals. The experiments aimed to investigate the potential of psychic abilities, specifically remote viewing, and to gather scientific evidence to support its validity.

Swann underwent a series of experiments in which he was asked to describe or sketch a remote place or thing that was selected randomly by the researchers. These locations and objects were typically outside the SRI building and unknown to Swann.

Swann's remote viewing sessions were conducted in a controlled environment, with measures taken to minimize the possibility of sensory input or other distractions that could influence his perceptions. The researchers recorded and analyzed Swann's descriptions and sketches of the remote targets to determine the accuracy of his perceptions.

The results of the SRI experiments were published in several scientific journals, including *Nature* and *Proceedings of the IEEE*. The experiments were met with both interest and skepticism from the scientific community. Some researchers praised the experiments as groundbreaking, providing evidence for the existence of psychic abilities, while others criticized the experiments as flawed and the results as inconclusive.

This research project was sponsored by the CIA and other governmental agencies interested in exploring the potential military and intelligence applications of psychic abilities. The project was part of a larger government initiative called the Stargate Project.

After leaving SRI and founding the Stanford Applied Research Institute, Targ and Puthoff continued their research on remote viewing. They continued to publish their findings and advocate for the scientific study of psychic phenomena. Despite the controversy, remote viewing has continued to be studied and practiced by individuals and organizations interested in exploring the potential of human consciousness. Some proponents believe that it has applications in fields such as law enforcement, medicine, and business.

Each supporter was well respected within their field, with William Crookes and Michael Faraday completely changing the scientific world with their most famous inventions, the Crookes Tube and the Faraday Cage. In addition, Osgood Mason was a noted physician and surgeon. At the same time, Wallace is most well known for having independently come up with the idea of evolution through natural selection.

So, with some of the brightest minds believing that clairvoyant travel could be possible, a sense of excitement was created within the spiritualist world as they waited for proof to be uncovered. These included many people who would even volunteer to participate in each figure's various tests.

Unfortunately, despite an exhaustive series of experiments in the years that followed, most of the scientific community would disregard the findings as nothing more than hearsay and conjecture. Even though in some of these studies, the scientists claimed to have obtained positive results to support the idea that traveling clairvoyance existed.

But in the end, this didn't seem to matter because the scientific world was not ready to recognize that something like this could be possible. It wouldn't be until the 1930s that the idea was broached more severely again, when noted American botanist and parapsychologist Joseph Banks Rhine began his research into the concept of traveling clairvoyance and telaesthesia.

Not wanting to have any of his work so easily dismissed as his predecessors, he built on what had been done by others in the past by taking their framework and expanding it to include larger sample sizes, something which he hoped would lend more credence to any results he was able to gather.

On top of that, he would also bring something new to the table in the form of a set of five cards, which he called Zener Cards. Each card contained one of five symbols: a square, a circle, a star, a plus sign, or a wavy pattern. Taking one of these cards, he'd hold it up facing away from his test subject, asking them to focus all their mental attention on the card and him as they tried to know the symbol.

After that, he would collate all the card guesses and see if the correct ones ended up being higher than one in five, the level which he deemed to be that of random chance. If it exceeded this percentage, he would classify the experiment as successful in showing that he could observe extra-sensory activity.

Where to Find More Information: Further Resources

If you want to see an example of this technique in action, it can be found in the opening scenes of the 1984 hit comedy Ghostbusters, when Peter Venkman, played by Bill Murray, tries out the test on a subject of his own. But just as in that movie, where Venkman's work would contribute towards him eventually being kicked out of the university he worked for, Rhine feared that his research would be equally as dividing once he presented it to his peers. That was why, despite gathering a lot of promising research over the next few years, he remained hesitant to publish it.

Instead, he'd bide his time as he continued working with several Duke University colleagues as they built up a portfolio of evidence through research on those who claimed to be remarkable. In 1934, he would finally feel confident enough to publish his work in a book called *Extra Sensory Perception*, which has since become a key text in the world of parapsychology.

How Remote Viewing Works

You can generate thoughts that create light waves with the universal mind. Your thoughts go out into space-time and interact with particles. "Entangle" refers to the process of becoming quantum entangled. All sentient beings can save and send information from universe to universe and galaxy to person.

ESP (Extrasensory Perception)

Most people call remote viewing a form of ESP or extrasensory perception. Everyone has ESP, which we are all born with. ESP is an often-unused part of our regulatory system.

Extrasensory perception is communication outside of standard sensory capabilities, as in telepathy and clairvoyance. The part of the brain activated during remote viewing sessions is called the neocortex. The neocortex (Latin for "new bark" or "new rind") is also called the neopallium ("new mantle"). It is part of the brain in mammals.

Scientific remote viewing (SRV) is a structured protocol for obtaining information about a distant or unseen target using only the power of the mind. Developed by researchers and practitioners in parapsychology, SRV aims to provide a systematic and verifiable method for accessing information beyond the limitations of time and space.

Practice Scientific Remote Viewing

When developing your remote viewing skills, you need an actual target you are viewing, and then you need to get feedback at the end of a session to compare your processes and the information detected to the target.

Here are the steps to understand and practice scientific remote viewing:

1. **Learn about remote viewing:** Familiarize yourself with the history, principles, and methodologies. There are numerous books, articles, and online resources available that provide an overview of the subject. Some notable authors and researchers include Ingo Swann, Russell Targ, and Joseph McMoneagle. You can also visit my website at www.jasonmedlock.com for a free consultation in remote viewing.
2. **Study the SRV protocol:** Scientific remote viewing follows a specific structure designed to minimize interference from the conscious mind and maximize the reliability of the information obtained. Learn the various stages of the SRV process, typically including:
    a. **Ideogram:** A spontaneous, abstract drawing representing the target.
    b. **Sensory impressions:** Describing colors, textures, shapes, smells, sounds, and temperatures related to the target.
    c. **Dimensional data:** Describing the target site's size, orientation, and spatial relationships.
    d. **Analytical data:** Making logical deductions or identifying patterns based on sensory and dimensional information.
    e. **Intuitive impressions:** Accessing higher-level information about the target, such as its purpose or meaning.
3. **Develop meditation and visualization skills:** SRV requires a clear, focused mind to access the subconscious mind and retrieve information. Practice meditation regularly to enhance your concentration, relaxation, and ability to quiet the mind. Develop your visualization skills, which will be crucial in remote viewing sessions.
4. **Practice with simple targets:** Start practicing SRV with simple, well-defined targets. These could include photographs, objects,

or locations you can access. Gradually increase the complexity of the targets as you become more proficient.
5. **Record your sessions:** Keep a detailed record of each remote viewing session, including the date, time, target, and impressions. Review your notes after each session to assess your perceptions' accuracy and identify improvement areas.
6. **Work with a partner or group:** Remote viewing can be more effective when practiced with others. A partner can provide feedback and support and help monitor your progress. They can also act as a "tasker," assigning targets and maintaining objectivity throughout the process.
7. **Analyze your results:** Assess the accuracy of your remote viewing sessions by comparing your impressions with the actual target. Identify patterns, strengths, and weaknesses in your viewing abilities. Use this feedback to refine your technique and improve your accuracy over time.
8. **Be patient and persistent:** Developing proficiency in scientific remote viewing takes time, practice, and dedication. Be patient with yourself and maintain a positive attitude as you work through the challenges and learning curves associated with this unique skill.
9. **Expand your knowledge:** Continue to study and learn from the experiences of others in the field of remote viewing. Attend workshops, conferences, or join online forums to connect with other practitioners and share your insights and experiences.
10. **Apply SRV to real-life situations:** As you become more confident in your remote viewing abilities, experiment with applying SRV to real-world problems, such as problem-solving, decision-making, or exploring historical events. These situations will help you hone your skills and demonstrate the practical applications of scientific remote viewing.

Lost Dog Found Through Remote Viewing

Let me give you an example of using scientific remote viewing to locate a distant object (in this case, a sentient being). One day I was called by a client who was frantic because she lost her dog. She urged me to help. To do this, I used a series of steps to reveal information from my subconscious mind and gave good enough detail about the area and eventual location of her missing dog.

I stated that the dog was in a wooded area, close to a water pond with a tent set up. I also saw a fence, power lines, and a tree- where I presumed the dog was napping. Once I gave this information to my client, she immediately said, "Oh my God! Oh my God! Jason, that is the area we just left." She sent me pictures of the area, just as I described.

Using remote viewing, the client's dog was found the next day, and wouldn't you know it—the dog was located under a fence; he was stuck and couldn't get himself free. This fence was next to the tree! This is a simple example of how this skill can help others in everyday life.

Associate Remote Viewing

I use Associate Remote Viewing a little differently. Associate Remote Viewing (ARV) is a variation of remote viewing that aims to predict the outcome of future events by associating each possible result with a distinct, unrelated target.

World-renowned professional Associate Remote Viewer David J. Wallace formally trained me. David taught me how to use carefully selected pictures, which you pick out yourself, to pull out meaningful numbers. Using ARV, I've successfully predicted the outcomes of NBA games, WNBA games, NFL games, golf tournaments, and anything I've ever been curious about.

Practice Associate Remote Viewing

David Wallace's book, *Picking Winners*, focuses on using ARV for predicting financial markets and sporting events. Here are the steps to understand and practice Associate Remote Viewing.

1. **Learn about remote viewing:** Familiarize yourself with the history, principles, and methodologies. Understand the differences between traditional remote viewing and Associate Remote

Viewing. You can book a consultation with me to gain insights into his specific approach to ARV at www.jasonmedlock.com.
2. **Choose an event to predict:** Select a future event with limited possible outcomes, such as a sports match or a financial market decision. Ensure that the result of the event is unknown at the time of the ARV session.
3. **Assign unique targets for each outcome:** Select an individual, unrelated mark that can be easily distinguished from the others for each possible event outcome. These targets, such as photographs, objects, or locations, should be simple and unknown to the remote viewer during the session.
4. **Develop a clear, focused mind:** Practice meditation regularly to enhance your concentration, relaxation, and ability to quiet the mind. A clear and focused mind is essential for successful remote viewing.
5. **Perform the ARV session:** Conduct a remote viewing session to perceive the target associated with the actual outcome of the event. Follow the remote viewing protocols and record your impressions; including sensory data, dimensional information, and intuitive insights.
6. **Interpret the results:** Review your recorded impressions after the session and determine which assigned targets your perceptions most closely match. The mark with the most decisive match represents the predicted outcome of the event.
7. **Verify the prediction:** Compare your predicted outcome with the product after the event. This will help you assess the accuracy of your ARV session and identify areas for improvement.
8. **Practice regularly:** Like any skill, ARV requires practice and dedication to develop proficiency. Regularly conduct ARV sessions to refine your technique and improve your accuracy.
9. **Record your sessions:** Keep a detailed record of each ARV session; including the date, time, event, assigned targets, impressions, and predictions. Review your notes to track your progress and assess the effectiveness of your ARV practice.
10. **Collaborate with others:** Connect with other remote viewers who practice ARV in person or through online forums. Share your experiences, insights, and techniques to enhance your

understanding of Associate Remote Viewing and learn from the experiences of others.

11. **Experiment with different events and targets:** As you gain confidence in your ARV abilities, experiment with predicting various events and using different types of targets. This will help you hone your skills and explore the potential applications of Associate Remote Viewing.

Using Subconscious Insights, I won

On March 15, 2022, I bet the over/under for the 76ers vs. Cavs; the o/u was 217. I asked my subconscious mind to reveal the picture representing the total combined score for the game being played that day. The image that was shown was a vacuum robot. I quickly started using my senses—sound, smell, taste, temperature, and sight. I matched the photo and counted how many of these senses I could directly associate with this image.

Once I made that determination, I took the number of senses and used a formula developed by Russell Targ. After my analysis, I determined that the points would go over 219. When the game was over, the total score was 232, resulting in a win!

Exploring the Enigmatic Skinwalker Ranch Through Remote Viewing

Utah's notorious Skinwalker Ranch has been called one of the world's most mysterious hot spots for UFO and "high strangeness" phenomena—including everything from mysterious animal deaths to hidden underground workings and possible gateways to other dimensions. Scientists and researchers have applied cutting-edge technology to investigate the 512-acre property to uncover the possibly "otherworldly" perpetrators behind it all.

In this remote viewing session, my goal was to uncover what is underneath the ground at Skinwalker Ranch and to discover what is causing the anomalies at the ranch. I performed a Type 6 RV session, meaning I received the information about my target before the session started.

The monitors of the session were me and my instructor, Tony Sivalelli. There are several phases and steps that I go through while gathering more information. As I apply psychic abilities through each stage, I slowly begin to develop a description of my target.

Phase 1

```
                              P1
Data: TYPE 6        PS - focused      ID: JASON MEDLOCK
Monitor: Jason/Tony  ES - Flat        Date: 7/19/2022
                    AP - Structures   Time: 5:10 PM


  5237                   IL: Energy, motion
  ----  {L             A: wiggly line going down
  1244

                       PD: S
                       AD: Artificial


                       B: water
                       C: Cold




                    " SKIN walker RANCH "
```

To begin the session, I started asking myself questions about my state of being. My *physical senses* seemed as focused as ever; this wasn't unusual since the target interested me. My *emotional reasons* were flat; I wasn't feeling too high or low. I was sort of in the middle. I did, however, have *advanced preceptors* of the target being a structure of some sort. Now that I had recorded how and what I was feeling, it was time to begin.

I proceeded to create target coordinates for Skinwalker Ranch. I picked target coordinates 5237 /1244 and repeated this number along with queuing my subconscious mind by repeating the following: What is under the ground at Skinwalker Ranch, located in the state of Utah? I repeated these numbers, 5237/1244, several times; that way, the information would be embedded in the ether of space, and all I would need to do is reference the coordinates and start to pull data from my subconscious mind.

As I was working through this remote viewing session, I started feeling energy—something constantly in motion. Whatever I was sensing was surrounded by a soft material or substance. This structure seemed artificial; I didn't understand that it had manufactured qualities. Several smooth edges don't have to adjourn bolts to keep the frame together. I thought water was present near this structure, which had a cold feeling.

Phase 2

Phase 2 consisted of many descriptors, which allowed me to probe deeper for my target's characteristics. I began by listening to *sounds* that were recognizable to me. I heard what sounded like a turbine engine turning. I also sensed what type of *textures* were present, I felt rock-like and surrounded by cold-like *temperatures*.

I got an overall visual of the *color*, which was black. The *luminosity* was dark, and there was a medium level of *contrast*. I then attempted to sense any type of *taste*, which seemed like iron to me. The *smells* of damp water were still present.

```
                                          P2

Sounds:  owls, Turbine Sound
TEXTURES : Rock
Temps :  Cold

Visuals →
                        Colors: BLACK
                        Lums: Dark
                        Contrasts: MEDIUM


Tates: Iron
Smells: Damp water
MAGS: →
                        Verticles - Tall
                        Horizontals - WIDE
                        Diagonals - slant
                        Topology - Round


Space, mass, Density & Volume: solid

Energetics: Spin

√F - Underground spinning Turbin Engines
```

I sensed the *magnitude* of this object. I sensed *verticals* that felt tall, and *extremely wide horizontals*. This object had a *diagonal* slant built into it, and when I smelled the *typology*, it was round. The space, mass, density, and volume of this 'object' seemed substantial; I sensed energy in and around it.

Phase 3

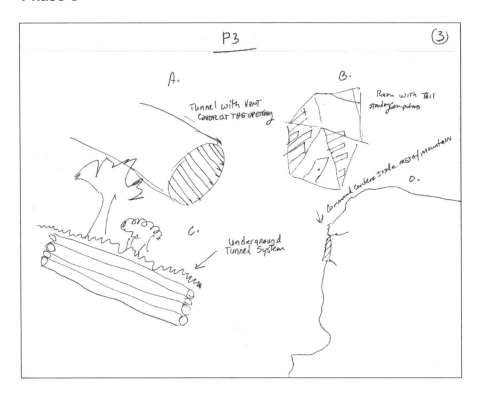

Entering phase 3, I typically try sketching one to four images I perceive. Simultaneously, I will ask my subconscious mind to show me the truth. "Show me what is underground at Skinwalker Ranch."

- A. My first impression was a vision of a large tunnel with a vent covering at the end of this tunnel.
- B. I looked deeper inside the facility/object and viewed a room full of towering computers.
- C. I sketched this image of several cylinder-shaped tunnel systems underground. I saw a tree and bushes above the ground.
- D. When the last image came to me, I was amazed. I saw the window of what appeared to be a command center. It looked like it was built into the mesa located on Skinwalker Ranch.

Phase 4

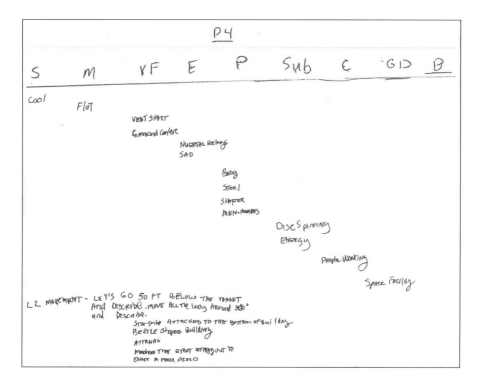

This part of my session allows me to probe even deeper into the characteristics of my target. I create a chart horizontally; I write out S (senses), M (magnitudes), VF (viewer feelings), E (emotions), P (physicals), Sub (subspace), C (concepts), GD (guided deductions), and D (deductions). These are senses I can use to extract more information about my target. Hopefully, I can use them to find out more about what's underground at Skinwalker Ranch.

I continued to *sense* a cold feeling, just as I did in the earlier phases. The *magnitude* of this object now seemed to be flat. I suddenly felt a *viewer feeling* of a vent shaft and a command center. I sketched both these images in phase three, so I wasn't surprised that I was sensing them again. I probed the *emotional* state of this location and felt neutral- maybe a being with no emotions or something to that effect, but I also lightly sensed the emotion of sadness.

While probing the *physical* aspects of the target, I got the impression of beings underground, steel material being used, several air vents, and the beings I sensed were human. Probing the *subspace* column while engaged in the session typically helps me determine if I feel something angelic, ghostly, positive, other-dimensional, or any type of movement. In this instance, I was able to see spinning discs underground that were surrounded by energy.

I then started to probe the *concept* column for a moment, and then it faded away; before it did, I saw people walking throughout this facility in the area I was viewing. I kept my mind in bliss before I probed the section-guided *deduction*. I don't want to taint it with my views, so typically, I'll put my pen down and then pick it back up to finish this part of the session. When I started probing this column, it came to me as soon as my pen hit the line: This was a space facility.

I still felt that there was more information, so I used additional SRV techniques to access this information. I decided to use a Level 2 movement, which allows me to get a closer look at the target. In this case, I knew there was a vast tunnel system below the ground, but what was at the end of this tunnel where I saw the vent covers? It was time for me to cue my subconscious once again for more answers.

L2-Movement allows me to move closer to the object I am viewing. Let's go 50 ft below the target and experience it.

I moved around the target 360 degrees to describe it. The images I saw were breathtaking. I saw an object with legs attached to the bottom of a circular building structure, reminding me of a giant beetle. The thing attached to the bottom of this structure appeared to be a smaller craft of some type. Several antennas were present, along with a machine that exerted energy that powers a translucent bubble (or dome-like) field.

The information coming through was fascinating. I decided to use an **L3 Movement** that allows me to go back and forth between prior knowledge that I sensed in previous phases, and what I was sensing in the present. The information below was recorded during phase 4 of my session. Using my intuition, I was able to detect a number of impressions that were all underground.

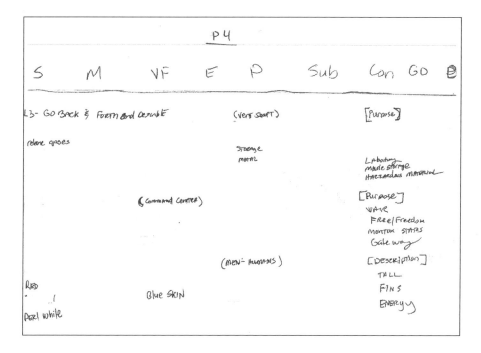

The **vent shaft** was used to release gasses, and a room made of some type of metal housed a laboratory, storing missile-looking objects and hazardous material.

The command center was the next piece of information coming through, and my goal was to understand its purpose. I immediately felt this facility was constructed as a war command center; I got the impression that this operation would be to free or create freedom for the inhabitants in the facility, monitor the universe, and control a gateway to our space.

The last intuition came when I sensed some type of being in the facility. I wanted a description of this being, so I began the process. They appeared to be tall, with fins. Some had blue skin, some had red skin, and others had pearl-white skin. I could sense a significant energy presence when viewing the pearl-white beings.

Phase 5

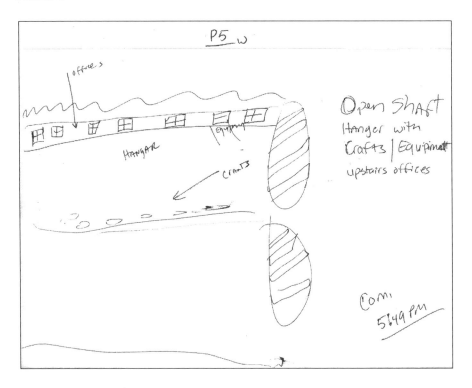

It became time for me to do one last sketch based on the additional information received in Phase 4. This time I got more insight into the target, and although I still felt like these were massive tunnels, I could view inside the facility and got the impression that there was a gigantic hangar that housed many crafts and equipment. I also viewed several window offices that overlooked the entire hangar.

Remote viewing is an incredible skill anyone can learn if they feel called to do so. Thank you for joining me on this journey of discovery, and for opening your heart and mind to the potential and possibilities of creation.

Chapter 7

The Art of Energy Healing

My Spiritual Teacher, Chloe Moers, was the first to introduce me to Galactic Energy Healing (GEH). I have enjoyed this healing method so much that I decided to follow in her footsteps and become a Certified Galactic Energy Healing Master. Galactic Energy Healing has enlightened my spirit and re-energized my being.

Galactic Energy Healing is a branch of energy healing, just like Reiki. Each branch of energy healing serves a unique and beautiful purpose. My sister is a Reiki practitioner, and I have interviewed countless Reiki masters to explore how this modality works.

Reiki Energy Healing: Earth-Based and Intuitive Approach

Reiki energy is a form of energy healing therapy. It is earth-based, not channeled through otherworldly beings. Sometimes it is intuitive, but oftentimes the healing is structured. Depending on the branch (as there are over 50 branches just in Reiki), Reiki primarily focuses on 3rd-dimensional healing for the body, mind, aura, and emotions in the present, past, and/or future.

Reiki was first awakened in Japan by Mikao Usui in the 1920s. In Japanese, Reiki translates to "universal life force energy." Reiki practitioners use palm healing or hands-on healing as a tool. In practice, life force energy is transferred through the palms of the practitioner to the patient to affect emotional and/or physical healing directly.

My first Reiki session was performed by a friend who, at the time, was a Reiki Practitioner and has since progressed to being a Reiki Master. I've always been fascinated by Reiki energy, so I tried it. My first session nearly put me to sleep from how relaxing it was.

Reiki has also been scientifically studied to quantify its effectiveness. A recent study by the Institute of Noetic Sciences (IONS) determined that Reiki energy increased greater well-being among study participants (the participants were previously experiencing varied medical issues). Improvement was noted for all participants, and the positive results continued days after the session.

If you are interested in receiving a Reiki session, you can search "Reiki practitioners near me" on Google, or you can explore the database of the International Association of Reiki Practitioners through their website: https://iarp.org/find-reiki-practitioner-teacher/ to find a qualified practitioner. Reiki sessions can be provided virtually or in person as energy goes beyond space and time. Chloe Moers also offers Reiki sessions of various branches, including Usui Reiki and Unconditional Love Reiki. Her website is www.magentasunhealing.com.

Galactic Energy Healing: Channeling Multi-Dimensional Beings

Galactic Energy Healing sessions are primarily done by channeling multi-dimensional beings; such as spirit guides, the consciousness of Mother Earth, Arcturians, Pleiadeans, Fendorians, Lyrans, higher selves, positive reptilians, and angels. Many powerful healing symbols were created by different beings from across the Universe and beyond.

When I first began learning to channel Galactic Energy Healing, I didn't know what to expect. I was already taking channeling lessons from my instructor, Chloe Moers. She performed an energy healing session on me before we started a channeling session, and it felt wonderful. This experience opened my eyes to the possibility that I could help others heal themselves.

I soon began my energy-healing journey. The Galactic Energy Healing methods were closer to what I had already practiced in my channeling classes, so I knew this would be a natural fit. I believe in sharing knowledge and experiencing things for myself, so let's quickly learn what I do when providing a session.

Grounding yourself is very important before providing an energy healing session. This is so you don't feel light-headed from the powerful energy; it also helps increase awareness during the session. I always ground myself first, then ground the person I'm providing the session for. I start this process by breathing in unconditional love and bright light, and exhaling all that I no longer need.

It is recommended to visualize grounding roots connecting you to the heart of Mother Earth, sending you healing and balancing nutrients through these roots. I also say words of gratitude towards myself and Mother Earth. This is how I typically ground myself; but sometimes I rinse my skin with cool water, drink or juice, walk, run, eat raw nuts, or stand barefoot.

It is important to call upon protection, love, guidance, and support from your higher self, spirit guides, the Universe, Mother Earth, and all the beings looking out for you. One intention I say is: "I truly unconditionally love and have beyond infinite gratitude for my higher self, my spirit guides, the Universe, Mother Earth—all of them and everything, including myself. I call upon protection, love, guidance, and support from all that look out for me."

Fifth-Dimensional Energy and Bright Light are channeled during my Galactic Energy Healing sessions, and this energy is pure and loving. This energy focuses on multi-dimensional healing in the physical form, spirit form, and soul form in the present, past, and/or future and works well for your emotions, mind, and aura. Channeled beings send and activate energy with intuitive and diverse healing methods. This energy can heal the mind, body, spirit, and soul; the therapeutic possibilities are unlimited.

So, what does it mean to "send" energy to someone? There are two parts, intention and action. First, you clarify your intention as positive, and for the greatest and highest love, for all involved. When something is truly what is best for you, then it is automatically what is best for everyone—even if they may not see it that way. Secondly, you initiate the action that sends and/or transmits the energy.

For example, when I send Unconditional Love Energy, I go through these two steps. First, I am really clear about my positive intention, which includes grounding myself and speaking the intention out loud. For example, I might say, "I call upon Unconditional Love Energy" with my palms facing the sky. Sometimes, I can feel the energy flowing through my hands- this feeling is amazing.

So, how is the energy "delivered"? When healing energy is sent to a person, the energy goes directly to the root cause of any imbalances they may have. This could be for healing inflammation or for balancing emotions, the mind, and releasing physical pain. It can also balance hormones, create peace, awaken love, and increase empathy. This energy is incredible for all life; animals, nature, and humans.

In preparation, I always clear my aura before a session by calling upon Bright Light Energy and Unconditional Love Energy, then send this energy to my aura for around two to five minutes. I do this daily or multiple times a day- whenever I feel overwhelmed, stressed, fearful, or anxious. When I am around those who are imbalanced, I know to cleanse myself after in a quiet space- to avoid absorbing other people's issues. Keeping your intentions and energy balanced is fundamentally important.

Galactic Energy Healing Symbols

There are more than ten energy healing symbols that can be channeled while providing a Galactic Energy Healing session. Typically, after I interview my client, I'll know which symbols are needed to complete the session or I will just intuitively use them. Unfortunately, I can't share them in this book as symbols are shared exclusively during sessions and classes for almost all branches of energy healing and Reiki.

Channeling the Energy

While I use several methods to connect and deliver energy, my favorite method is to *channel through the heart space*. When I'm ready to begin a session; I call upon protection, love, guidance, and support, followed by a simple breathing exercise. Once that is complete, I imagine myself standing at the top of my crown chakra and walking downstairs, on a slide, or an elevator until I reach the door to enter my heart space (located in the center of the heart chakra). I know there is a beautiful space beyond the door that I will choose, or my higher self will choose, once I enter and explore.

Once inside, I invite the beings I wish to channel and communicate with. This usually takes me a few minutes. Once ready, I ask the being/s to merge with the chakras in my body while I remain in my heart space. I allow the beings to move through my body for energy healing. I then relax and trust in the process.

After every session, I do a grounding exercise for myself, set my intention to be disconnected from whomever I am channeling, and watch them fade away. I sweep and close my aura and the aura of whomever I was sending energy to, unless it was for Mother Earth herself (as her aura can remain open). I continue to share gratitude and love for all beings, the universe, the energy, and myself. Gratitude and love keep the vibration high and are powerful for protection, positive manifestation, and healing.

One of the best parts of learning GEH is that you get to administer energy healing for yourself. I once performed a session on myself to decrease pain in my elbow, which was successful. I started searching for different types of energy to connect with that would relieve this pain. For my first session (on this issue), I went into my heart space and asked positive beings, "What type of Healing Chamber would serve me the highest?"

For the second session that was provided for this purpose, I had another practitioner assist. Chloe called upon custom Galactic Flower Seeds and asked for the seeds to be planted inside my elbow or wherever it would be beneficial. Chloe then asked these flowers to bloom and activate when I needed them and sent fifth-dimensional energy to the seeds. After that, I set my intention that the healing chamber and custom Galactic Flower Seeds would be created for the greatest and highest good possible. The inflammation in my elbow decreased rapidly!

Energy healing includes a range of powerful methods for a variety of purposes. May you connect with a modality of energy work that resonates with you and may you feel the benefits of it.

Chapter 8

Exploring the Subconscious Mind

The subconscious mind is one of the most incredible aspects of the human brain, and it's been a critical factor in our evolution on Earth. It helps us get through each day by dedicating thought space to things we wouldn't be able to otherwise, and for that reason alone, it's worthy of further discussion. We will go in-depth about how and why it works the way it does because once you understand this, how humans operate shall make greater sense.

What is the Subconscious Mind?

The subconscious mind operates behind the conscious layer of awareness, usually carrying out processes that are, in some ways, automatic and unknown. Why does it do this? Carrying out these functions without being consciously told to, leaves more time and space to consciously focus on other things - without feeling overwhelmed by so much information all at once.

Your mind would overflow with sensory information, making it nearly impossible to remember all the pertinent information correctly. That's where the subconscious mind comes in.

When driving, we don't need to think about every aspect of driving, such as how to turn the wheel or turn on an indicator, as our subconscious mind already has this information stored and will activate it automatically when needed. Likewise, you won't struggle to remember how to ride a bike, even if you haven't for several days or months. Our body remembers through the subconscious mind.

Some might consider this solely muscle memory, but the work of the deeper level of our mind stores learned information (Ref 1). But how did we discover this excellent function within our minds, and how has our understanding of it developed over time? To explain this, we'll now explore the history of humans and the subconscious.

Unveiling Ancient Subconscious Insights

Human understanding of the subconscious likely dates back to the earliest civilizations. Back then, the concept may have been a lot more interchangeable with what we now understand as the unconscious mind, another level of our brains that we'll get to in a moment.

Imagine the Incas or the Mesopotamians as they listened to the words of 'gods' in their heads, telling them what to do. In truth, this could have been their internal thoughts instructing them to carry things out in a way that was the safest and most beneficial for their evolutionary success.

So, if it's been part of our understanding, at least to some degree, for all this time, then why did it take so long to be fully codified into words? Honestly, it could have already been (long ago) but then forgotten, hidden, or disappeared. But based on our current understanding and knowledge, we didn't have the right words or level of understanding to explain the phenomenon until the 1800s.

That was when Pierre Janet, a French psychologist, physician, and philosopher, first coined the term 'subconscious' when looking for something to describe the connection he'd noticed between one of his patient's current-day traumas and their past experiences. The way he saw it, two minds were operating simultaneously, one below the surface. And what was happening at the time had no power over that mind. (Ref 2)

As groundbreaking an idea as this was, it didn't fully breach the mainstream's attention until a few years later, when the famed father of modern psychology, Sigmund Freud, furthered the concept by coming up with the iceberg theory of the mind. And in this, he explained that there were three layers of our thoughts: the conscious one above the water line, followed by the preconscious, and the unconscious below this underneath the surface.

It should be noted that when Freud spoke of the preconscious, he referred to what we understand today as the subconscious, which contains thoughts and feelings the individual is not necessarily consciously aware of- but can be brought to conscious awareness if needed. Again, let's take the analogy of driving to work. You might find yourself suddenly in a situation where you need to take an unexpected detour. At this point, all your knowledge about operating a vehicle will soon return to the surface as you navigate a new path you may not be familiar with.

Of course, that's only a basic description of Freud's theory, and we'll explore it in more detail in a moment. But as a general summary, according to Freud, the subconscious mind contains a whole reservoir of crucial information that we use to help us get through our daily lives, and it is constantly working behind the scenes, even if we aren't aware of it doing so.

More than just being a simple aid to help us get through the day, Freud understood it as the primary source of human behavior. Like an iceberg, you see, the most essential part of the mind is the part you cannot visibly observe. (Ref 3). Because of the popularity of his theories in the mainstream, knowledge of the subconscious mind and its power quickly became something the whole world was aware of, to the point that today it's just something we take for granted as common knowledge.

Subconscious and Unconscious: Revealing Differences

As we mentioned before, most of our understanding of the subconscious mind, at least from the past few hundred years, came from the work of

Sigmund Freud and his Iceberg Theory. As a recap, he was the one who explained the mind in three parts, with the two below the surface being the preconscious (or subconscious) and the unconscious.

We've described the subconscious already, so let's briefly investigate how the unconscious differs. Rather than acting as an automated part of the brain that carries out necessary functions without the need for direct instructions, the unconscious is more of a pool of past experiences that are inaccessible to the other parts of the mind as they may be too traumatic or damaging to be allowed to come to the surface. (Ref 3)

Of course, for his work as a psychotherapist, this was a crucial element of the iceberg for Freud, as it allowed him to access things that may serve as the root causes of people's problems. But, for the sake of the purpose of this book, let us further explore scientific research carried out on the subconscious mind over the years.

Specifically, we will look at a 2015 study by Noriya Watanabe and Masahiko Haruno that sought to observe how the subconscious and conscious minds each reacted to being asked to recognize subtle differences in facial expressions. For this experiment, they presented participants with a series of human faces in rapid succession. Then they were asked to determine whether the facial expressions in the previous picture mimicked the same emotion.

This was much easier to do when those pictures were changed slowly, precisely every 0.047 seconds, as the conscious mind could keep up with it. But when things were sped up a little, to the level of 0.027 seconds, things got a lot more complex, and the subjects found it significantly harder to tell if there was any noticeable difference.

What does this tell us, then? The conscious and subconscious minds both take in information and process it differently. For example, the conscious mind can look at something, take stock of what's there, and then apply this knowledge.

When things move quicker, though, and the subconscious mind is forced to kick in, we find that such new information cannot be processed so quickly. As we mentioned before, this part of our mind is one that, in many ways, works on an automatic level and must be conditioned with information for some time before it can utilize it correctly. (Ref 4)

Again, returning to the analogy of driving a car; the first time you do it, your subconscious hasn't had a chance to learn what's happening yet, so it can't help you. But once it's allowed to learn, it can be far more potent than perhaps any other part of the mind. This has been shown in recent brain imaging research, which delves into the depth of thought going on. At the same time, the subconscious is activated much more significantly than any other part of the brain (Ref 3).

It's quite remarkable that this is all happening beneath the surface. Of course, even today, we still must learn much more about the mind and its operation, so you could argue that our current knowledge is still primitive. But what we can be sure of is that the subconscious mind has plenty of valuable benefits if you harness its power.

Potential Benefits

While it primarily operates independently, the conscious mind can significantly harness the subconscious to benefit an individual's daily life. Before we delve into this, let us explore how it can be beneficial, starting with its power to give someone an overall better memory. If the subconscious holds so much information that we don't usually have access to, then accessing it will provide us with more data to use. And if you struggle with remembering things, then using the increased memory function of this part of your brain could be invaluable.

On top of that, the more knowledge we can draw from our subconscious minds, the greater the ability we should have to find solutions to problems. We have a whole ocean of knowledge just beneath the surface. If we can utilize this knowledge to its fullest potential, our problem-solving ability should be increased tenfold.

Doing this could increase our creative abilities, allowing us to do things we might never have dreamed possible. There's even the potential increase in empathy we could feel towards others of all species because of a better understanding of them. We'll theoretically be able to put ourselves in their being much easier.

There are even more potential benefits from harnessing the power of the subconscious mind! Aside from enhancing our creativity, we can also improve our learning abilities, all while developing better overall clarity of thought, and even a better understanding of any root fears that prevent us from living a full life. (Ref 5)

The positives we could take from this are almost endless, and with our understanding of the subconscious growing daily, that potential only increases. But how can you start the process of harnessing these powers for yourself? Let's find out.

Unlocking the Power of the Subconscious Mind: A Journey to Success, Intuition, and Self-Discovery

From the moment I lay my head on a pillow to the instant I awaken to experience a new day, I program my subconscious mind for success, wealth, and health. This harmonious relationship between my conscious and subconscious mind allows me to thrive daily. I rely on my willpower and the conviction that I can achieve anything I want to maintain a steady balance between my conscious and subconscious mind. As a professional remote viewer, I consistently utilize my subconscious mind to reveal hidden targets and predict future events. I also use my subconscious mind to address simple life questions.

Transcendental meditation (TM) is my daily meditation method, which helps me to communicate effectively with my subconscious mind about my goals and aspirations. One day, after a peaceful meditation session, I attempted to use my subconscious mind to predict the outcome of an NBA game. Initially, I was uncertain if I could access my subconscious mind for such a purpose. Nevertheless, I began my preparation by meditating briefly and making my subconscious mind aware of my intentions. After going through a series of Associate Remote Viewing steps, I felt ready to place my bet.

I wagered $50 on my first prediction, and the Lakers covered the over. I won $47. The money wasn't important; the bet demonstrated the potential of the subconscious mind to enhance various aspects of life. I routinely use this powerful tool to describe remote targets using eight digits as clues. I use my subconscious mind when making business decisions, asking it to reveal the truth about potential transactions. Often, my subconscious mind makes a decision before my conscious mind can intervene.

I've also utilized my subconscious mind to choose vacation destinations by listing three or four places I'd like to visit. The practice of Associate Remote Viewing allows me to use my subconscious mind to answer this question. After performing a series of steps, the answer becomes clear. People often ask me if I find this ability mind-blowing, but my response remains consistent: I have trained my subconscious mind to share the truth about what I seek. Through regular positive self-talk and confronting negative thoughts, I've honed my ability to connect with my subconscious mind.

This isn't a special gift reserved only for me (it is accessible to everyone), and a constant struggle still exists between my destructive and constructive thoughts. I can create my desired reality by maintaining consistency and allowing my constructive thoughts to prevail. The power of the mind enables us to experience all levels of existence. Embracing constructive ideas raises our vibration, ultimately enhancing our connection with our higher selves.

Elevate Your Mind for Success

Before going any further, removing any skeptical parts of your thought process and shifting your thinking into that of a wholehearted believer is essential. Let's make no mistake here. The subconscious mind is real. Be willing to see that seemingly unchangeable part of yourself change, visualize it, and know that you've already carried out the most challenging part once you've done that.

Once that is complete, it's time to allow yourself to be successful. Too often in life, our fears and insecurities keep us from achieving what we're fully capable of. But if we can overcome this and set ourselves on a path where success is not only achievable but likely, then we've broken through a formidable barrier.

This might sound like manifestation or meditation, because it is. Many of these processes are closely interlinked, so it should come as no surprise that there's some overlap in how we practice them.

It is also essential to not allow the fears of others to influence you. For example, consider how others might react to an engagement announcement. Those already in happy relationships will likely feel pleased and offer congratulations. Those who are in unhappy relationships may provide warnings about the future.

The key is not to let those negative ideas halt you from achieving your goals. And, of course, this doesn't necessarily have to be about an impending marriage. It can be about anything. Perhaps you want to harness the power of your subconscious mind to help you change your career path, or maybe you want to heal your body.

Either way, the point remains: reduce negativity and surround yourself with positive reinforcement to help you reach your goal. In addition, when talking about your goal, please don't speak of it as a plan you have for the future. Think of it as a present fact—something you're actively engaged in and have already achieved. "I am healthy in mind, body, and spirit." "I have the job that resonates with me." Talk about it as if you've already done it.

We've shared a lot about getting your head in a suitable space, so now it's time to do something more tactile by creating a vision space for whatever you want to achieve. This can be done on a vision board, a notebook, or anything else you have available. The important thing isn't the item used; it's the fact that you utilize it to create a crystal-clear image of where you see yourself going.

In addition, having a gratitude journal that will help you change your thought process and uplift your spirit can also be invaluable. If you do these steps, you'll soon see that this all seems more achievable. It might not seem like you're utilizing your subconscious mind at any point here, but you are. After all, this is not a part of the mind that operates on the surface, but instead learns and is trained through the actions of the conscious mind. As we're consciously working on these changes, we're effectively retraining our subconscious to act differently, giving us greater access to the wealth of information it has whenever we need it.

You don't have to overanalyze this process. Often, great things fall into our laps in a way we could never have anticipated. And if we're harnessing the power of our subconscious, it will do a lot of the work in helping us get where we want to be. At this point, you should focus on surrounding yourself with allies who can help you achieve your goals, while constantly affirming a positive attitude. Keep yourself in that mindset; before you know it, your subconscious should work remarkably for you. (Ref 6)

Further Resources for Deeper Understanding

If what you've heard so far has engaged your interest and you want to do more research on the subject in your own time, there is a wealth of information out there. Most of this information can be found online through a simple Google search. But, if you're looking for specific recommendations for more information, we'd recommend starting with the American Psychological Association. This organization has done much work on everything involved in the human mind, not just the subconscious. (Ref 7)

If you're based in the UK, there's also the British Psychological Society- a similarly structured group. (Ref 8). In addition to these resources, there's the INLP Center, which offers much information on the subconscious mind and how to harness it to improve your life. (Ref 9). There are countless sources available, so all you must do is put the intention out there, and quickly, you should find precisely what you're seeking.

Empower Your Mind's Potential

The power of your mind is just sitting there, waiting for you to unlock it. Know that you're not the only one going on this journey. It is your birthright to unlock your potential. Millions of people worldwide are also trying to use their subconscious minds to better both themselves and the lives of others. You're not alone on this path. There are plenty of online forums to share your experiences with such people, which we recommend if you're starting. But ultimately, whether you choose to do this or not, the essential thing is that you enjoy the process. Don't let it overwhelm you or intimidate you. Know that the work you're starting today will be well worth it.

To conclude, let's look at some additional exercises you can attempt at home to unlock the power of the subconscious mind. We've already discussed using positive affirmations to help you on your journey and how similar the process is to meditation. But, we still need to discuss how to apply this positivity to others around us. We can affirm ourselves and our goals, while spreading excess energy to all of Earth. Through the power of intention, we can help not just ourselves but everyone else.

Doing this will further deepen your connection with your subconscious mind and help you get to where you need to be all the quicker. To speed up the process, you can also try automatic writing—putting pen to paper and etching down something without thinking about what you are doing. The more you do this, the more you tap into your subconscious mind. And in doing so, you will find thoughts and feelings you may not have known you had. This is an excellent way of quickly tapping into that side of yourself, just as listening to your dreams can also be an invaluable source of information.

That's precisely why you should keep a dream journal to remember the things going through your mind while you sleep at night, because our dreams may very well be the purest representation of our subconscious minds. So, why wouldn't we want to listen to them and see what they have to share? Again, this doesn't require much effort; you only need a pen and paper by your bedside. (Ref 10)

We hope this will start you on your path toward unlocking your subconscious mind. We wish you all the best in your journey and hope it takes you to places greater than you could have ever imagined.

Chapter 9

Channeling - Opening the Door to Higher Consciousness

Channeling is a captivating and transformative practice that enables individuals to connect with higher levels of consciousness; such as spirit guides, angels, spirits, higher-selves, and even divine beings. Through meditation and heightened awareness, channeling can facilitate personal growth, spiritual development, and a deeper understanding of the universe.

The Foundation: Meditation and Centering

Meditation is at the core of channeling, cultivating mental clarity, inner peace, and heightened awareness. Whether seeking to connect with spirits, deities, deceased loved ones, interdimensional beings, or healing energies, a strong foundation in meditation is essential for successful channeling.

Like any skill, channeling requires practice and dedication. Spiritual practices, such as manifesting or remote viewing, are built upon a solid foundation of meditation. By calming the mind, harmonizing the breath, and reaching a profound, centered state, practitioners can more effectively open themselves to higher vibrations and energies.

Developing Your Channeling Practice

As you develop your channeling practice, it is essential to cultivate an open and receptive mind, which will allow you to attune to higher vibrations and energies more easily. Regular meditation, mindfulness exercises, and energy work can help you achieve this state.

When you begin channeling, focus on setting clear intentions and establishing a safe and sacred space for communication with higher consciousness. This may involve creating a calming environment, using crystals or other energy-enhancing tools, and setting boundaries to protect yourself from negative energies.

As you progress in your channeling practice, remain patient and open to the messages and guidance you receive. Remember that channeling is a deeply personal and unique experience; your journey may not look like someone else's. Trust your intuition and embrace the insights you gain, as they can contribute to your personal growth, spiritual development, and overall well-being.

Clearing Your Vessel: Preparing the Body, Mind, and Emotions

Before attempting to channel, it is crucial to clear and balance your vessel, which involves preparing your physical body, mind, and emotions for communication with higher consciousness. One aspect of cleansing yourself is maintaining a high-vibrational diet, as what you consume can directly impact your ability to connect with spiritual realms.

Low-vibrational foods, such as processed or animal-based products, can hinder your ability to channel effectively. Instead, opt for high-vibrational, natural foods that are raw and grown from the earth, such as fruits, vegetables, nuts, and seeds. It is also important to refrain from lab-made drugs and alcohol. These nourishing choices can help raise your energy and vibration, preparing you for successful channeling.

Channeling is a powerful practice that can provide profound insights, guidance, and healing. By dedicating time and effort to meditation, maintaining a high-vibrational lifestyle, and cultivating an open and receptive mindset, you can unlock the door to higher consciousness and enhance your spiritual journey. Embrace the transformative potential of channeling and discover the infinite wisdom that awaits you.

Understanding Channeling from My Teacher *Chloe Moers*

After interviewing renowned channeler Chloe Moers, my main objective was to understand how this process began for Chloe and prepare myself to undergo the necessary training to experience this remarkable phenomenon properly. Channeling can happen consciously or subconsciously, and everyone has the innate ability to channel. Most people channel daily with their intuition and receive ideas that come to them from higher sources.

There are different channeling and communication forms; most people experience channeling daily without knowing it. For instance, some of the songs that have been written and streamed all over the world have been channeled—either consciously or subconsciously—from multi-dimensional beings. You might find this hard to believe, but we must consider that music is a universal language. Some people have even shared that during a near-death experience, they could clearly hear fulfilling beautiful music while entering the light.

There are many ways to channel. In addition to verbal channeling; you can channel write, create, paint, and feel. A being, consciousness, energy, spirit, or individual can come through your chakras and physical form, providing you with various feelings and sensations.

Chloe can, for instance, connect to an elephant and feel what it is like to be them. She channels emotions through clairsentient abilities. Chloe shared with me that she figured out how to do this at about 14 years of age, but before then, she was still channeling naturally and intuitively in everyday life- like most individuals.

One who witnesses channeling in this form might believe those who can induce such communication must be unique or possess superpowers, but anybody can do it. Of course, you must awaken your potential, practice, and prepare.

Chloe said, "Many of my clients and people who come to me have never channeled themselves consciously, but this is a common question where people will ask whether this is something they can do or is this something that only selected individuals can do. Anyone can perform channeling; you have to tune into your body. It takes practice, just like anything else you want to achieve."

All people have this ability, regardless of age or background, which manifests uniquely. It's just the amount that they're willing to tap into that makes the difference. As humans, we also share other capabilities, such as telepathy, which uses the third eye chakra and the heart space, located in the heart chakra- locations also essential for channeling.

It is important to trust yourself and be open-minded. As a young boy, I heard people shouting, screaming, and speaking intensely in church. I did not know what they were doing or what to think, and I remember my mom would say things like, "Oh, Sister Johnson just got happy. The Lord touched her spirit." My experiences in the church helped me be more open and curious about channeling as an adult. As I gained more knowledge in spirituality, I realized that when you reach the height of worship where God speaks to you, you tap into a frequency that allows you to have this clairaudient experience.

Vibration makes all the difference when channeling. I've met channelers who live a less-than-perfect lifestyle. They may have to meditate for hours before channeling. Eating healthy foods and avoiding animal products and processed foods typically connect much easier and faster.

Some channelers can connect to another realm in just one or two minutes. Chloe can begin fully channeling within 2 minutes, which is considerably quicker than many others. On the topic, Chloe said, "Honestly, this is not something that just happened. It's like any skill. It takes time to build up to this point. It's about trusting in oneself, but what you put in your body is important, and fruit is the highest vibrational food that one can put in their body." Remember, your body will help you achieve contact when cared for lovingly. Learn to balance your ego, transcend fear, and clear a path for mindfulness and personal evolution.

Channeling Session "Live" with Jason Medlock

Here is a partial transcript from a channeling session where we communicated with a group of spiritual beings called the Collective:

The Collective: Knowing that love is within you is essential. You can always connect to love without love surrounding everything, everyone, and every place. Love is within you. When you always have love within you, it keeps your body moving and keeps you alive. When someone has no attachment within them, they will transition out of this world. When love finally leaves them, they will go, regardless of age.

People can also leave this lifetime intentionally. Death should always be by intention and should never be an accident, and know that it is never an accident, even if it seems like it is. Death is not something to fear. It's just as beautiful and as magical as birth; it needs to be talked about, something that needs to be embraced. Also, you must connect to love daily. This will inspire you and connect you to your mission and life.

When you complete your mission in life, you will feel joy no matter what is happening; no matter if you're going through loss, tragedy, heartache, or different challenging things to go through in life, you will feel an imbalance. Yes, it may be problematic. Sadness is an important emotion to feel repeatedly, so yes, these challenges may be complex, but you will be in balance, and this balance will keep you moving forward.

To unlock this love with you, there are different ways to do it. One way is gratitude; connecting to gratitude will automatically spark love within you. You can also call upon it the same way people call upon energy, prayer, and connection from their higher self or the angels. You can say, "I connect upon this pure unconditional love within me, and I asked for this love to come out to spread around me to fill my aura, to fill my body, my mind, my emotions, my spirit, my soul, and I ask this love to flood my life for infinite love.

You can pull love out or set the intention and allow it to flow out like a river naturally, but it's essential not to look at this just from the outside. You can get it from nature, you can get it from the sky, you can get it from each other, but it will always feel like something that keeps on escaping or moving like the wind. It will feel continuous, solid, powerful, and mesmerizing when you get it from your inner self.

You are very mesmerizing inspirational beings; connect to this feeling. Just let yourself flow. You will always be supported when you let who you are flow into the universe. You don't have to worry about those minor inconveniences because it will always come back into a full circle of love. This is the message I must share. Are there any questions?

Jason: Yes, I'd like to understand the purpose of our incarnation on Earth. We are here to learn, but how do we channel otherworldly beings? How do we get into our spiritual man? How do we start to live a better, cleaner life while incarnated on Earth?

The Collective: On Earth, people lack proper attachment; people have too much passion for convenience, other individuals, and a particular way of life.

Yet when someone gives up attachment, they allow change, allowing themselves to move with life and be more in tune with the Earth. When people are attached to certain things in their diet or lifestyle, they will not connect to the highest vibration.

Many people are unwilling to give up things—like meat or alcohol, for instance—because they are attached to them. Once they give up this attachment, they connect to fruit and living foods. They will feel much more powerful and connected to their mission and helping Earth.

Everyone here on Earth has a collective mission to unite, have a global ecosystem with everyone, and define a proper, unconditionally loving balance where no one is getting hurt; no one is getting trampled on for another to reach the top. There is a perfect ability to have balance and harmony throughout all life, so this is achievable, but it must be through letting go of attachments.

Channeling Energy Healing Session

I am including energy healing sessions in this chapter because my instructor, Chloe Moers, uses channeling during our healing sessions. Chloe began the first session by reading my oracle cards (she doesn't typically do this during a session, but felt called to this time). I'd never had my cards read before and was very interested in hearing what she had to say. After my card reading, we jumped right into my energy healing session.

Session 1

Chloe: So basically, we will focus on physical movement, allowing your body to flow naturally, and doing different forms of anything based on hands-on physical training. The next card I got is persistence, so this is just not giving up; knowing that you're on the right track, you're moving forward, taking the necessary steps, in tune with your mission, and where you need to be.

Just let go of any expectations because things work in a specific time frame because time is very relevant. So just listen to your body, mind, and feelings, and know that what you are viewing and experiencing in the visions you are picking up have full relevance. You are learning here how to interpret, work with, listen, and allow your abilities to engage naturally. Your knowledge will increase overnight, and there can be an energy upgrade or a transition within your body, mind, spirit, and soul when you're asleep.

One day you will wake up, and you'll automatically have knowledge of a new ability, so listen to yourself if you suddenly feel guided, even if you're doing something or are busy. So, if you feel directed at this moment, ground yourself and say, "I want to do this exercise or this meditation or this energy work," and then go for it.

Listen, follow your intuition, focus on yoga, different physical or energy exercises, going outside, having persistence, not giving up, also at the same time, letting go of your expectations of things because we all are very different; we all have different abilities, and while some of us have similar skills, we process things differently.

Just continue forward from there and choose peace with yourself. Sometimes we can get a little aggravated at ourselves, like, "I should be able to do this already," or "Why am I able to do this but not that?" And so just continuing to choose peace within yourself and knowing that all unfolds with divine timing. Do you have any questions before I connect to the Pleiadian individual?

Jason: Umm, on what you just covered?

Chloe: Yes.

Jason: No, no, no.

The Collective: It's time to connect to star energy. There are many, many, many different stars, as you're aware, and each has its unique energy; each flows in its unique and beautiful way when you connect to these energies. As a whole consciousness, the stars are individuals.

Yes, they're individual balls of energy, but they connect as a consciousness intertwined. When you connect and channel this consciousness, things will be a lot more activated. With this comes a form of patience; you won't need to have any more in the same way because, of course, patience will come up in different forms in life, but the specific patience, you won't have to have any more.

Things will start to flow more smoothly, quickly, and in tune with who you are. You know who you are. You are developing your abilities. You're developing who you are as an individual, not just in this lifetime but in every lifetime and soul and spirit and who you are in the origins you are connecting to your consciousness in the global consciousness as well.

A lot of what you've been working on and focusing on and building, even when you may not notice the full results in the conscious mind, it's already being engaged within your being. You are already evolving with everything you learn, everything you do, and every exercise you complete makes a huge difference within your being.

Recognizing this is very important, and have gratitude for your being and for how you've been moving forward because you're moving forward in the right way, this will be an instant moment, sometimes with progress. There is conscious progress and awareness progress, but it will be an instant moment when you absorb all that you've done in this time. It'll be an instant moment where you will have different realizations and where the pieces will all come together, but you're doing well. You're on the right path.

I will now connect you to the star consciousness energy. I will fill it within your form; once I do that, I'm creating a direct channel from it to you, and all you must do is say, "I connect, I engage, and I absorb this direct star consciousness channel." That's all you must say, and you can say it in any form that resonates with you. This ensures that you're fully absorbing and connecting, and reflecting on this energy. Think of this energy as a spirit that guides the ultimate higher self for you.

This would be guidance, this would be intuition, this would be activation, and they will help you interpret what you do experience, and they will help you have more and more intricate and vivid visions.

They will help you connect your abilities and use them to their full extent. The energy will be powerful and will help you through this process. Do you have any questions about anything, anything at all? I'm happy to help before we begin.

Jason: I was having some problems connecting, so I asked myself what I could do to connect, and you just answered my question.

However, I do have one question. Through my show *The Expansion of Consciousness*, I've been sharing information with the masses or whomever would accept this knowledge. I'm trying to get more high-level consciousness people viewing so I can share. I want to be able to share with a much bigger audience. How do I do that?

The Collective: By reaching out to other platforms. Reach out to people doing things similarly but different to what you're doing. Make connections and build community. These are not your competitors. These are your friends. These are communities. These are individuals who also want to achieve similar goals.

Reach out to them and make more collaborations with other businesses, companies, organizations, individuals, and people who are doing something similar but not the same. If it's the same, that could get a little bit odd. But, for instance, it could be another podcast. It could be a different outreach group. It can be many different individuals, but with a similar idea of what they wish to achieve. Collaborations. You can share content with one another, which will help build things up.

Naturally, the collaboration will create positive manifestation, creating even more of a global community and global listeners. This will happen even if you don't do this because people are sharing what you're doing with one another, creating a chain reaction of people who are aware of that, and people who wish to participate. You're ready for collaboration and reaching out to others. I'm hoping this new energy will help people to trust you.

The big issue that this world has is the humans of this world. Many of them don't trust one another, and they get scared of collaboration, sometimes in the subconscious mind, because they think it could create some form of competition.

This is naturally within many humans because they are mammals, and they're focused on survival, but in general, everyone must collaborate and work with one another. This is how consciousness reunites, and what the world desperately needs is reunited consciousness, so the information you're putting out is very valuable.

Be careful to make sure that you like the individuals you interview or work with. If something doesn't feel fully right, do not put it out to the world. Even if it may feel a little too late, it's never too late; this is important information for you to only work with those who resonate with you. Do you have any other questions?

Jason: No.

The Collective: For this healing, hold this position in a way that feels comfortable and relaxed but allows the energy to flow. What you are doing by holding this position is naturally inviting energy to flow within your energy channel and within yourself, so hold this position for the duration of energy healing, and I'm going to begin now. I wish you enjoyment and will let you know once it is complete.

The energy healing process is done, but now the Tree of Stars continues to form around you for the next ten days. I connected you to this energy from the stars from each direction from their consciousness.

Your cells were receptive and absorbing their power. Your channel accepted their glow. I must share something exciting; usually the Tree of Wisdom does not choose to grow around an individual. With the Tree of Wisdom with the foundation of Starlight surrounding you, Jason, this will continue to form for the next 10,000 years.

There will be different lifetimes, and while you are just residing in your spirit form as well, you're going to become this tree at the end of these 10,000 years. You're going to be able to give to others in a way that is not yet fully understood. Still, for now, the tree is growing. Allow the tree to grow.

It will work with you; it will boost your energy, boost your abilities, and give you flights in this lifetime. It's an extraordinary form of it. Ten days from now, exactly ten days from now, at the time of 11:11, I ask you to make a wish, but be careful. The wish you can plan out beforehand or say intuitively on the spot. This is up to you.

Create a wish. This wish will have a lot of manifestation power ten days from now at 11:11, whether it's during daylight or nighttime. This is irrelevant; use the power. Channel it, call upon this star consciousness, call upon this tree at any point that will reside with you, and your abilities will manifest in a way you didn't know was possible, but be patient and follow your intuition. You know how to move forward; you've had so many lifetimes of wisdom.

What are your questions? Do you have any more or anything you wish to say now that the Collective is listening?

Jason: This tree of wisdom, will I become the tree, or the tree surrounds me?

The Collective: The tree surrounds you now, but it's forming its energy right now. It's manifesting around you, which will take around ten days. Ten thousand years from now, you will merge and become this tree until you grow with it. This tree has a lot of power. It comes from all directions and transcends time and space. It knows, and it sees, and it understands, you'll be able to tell if someone's soul is fragmented, and the tree will be able to repair it with you. Do you have any other questions?

Jason: I feel held back and feel surrounded in this 3D world, trying to survive it. In this world sometimes I feel like all that I love to do I keep being pulled away from. Pulled away from what I love the most, and that's to share knowledge and connect with others like me. What can I do to remove these feelings?

The Collective: It's remembering that this is temporary and setting the intention of letting go of this feeling. Your life will shift automatically, things will take off, and you will be able to leave a lot of 3D worlds behind and pursue more knowledge and greater understanding and share with others full-time.

You're transitioning to this right now. Just think of things like a transition period. There's nothing wrong, and it's not holding you back. Just have patience with yourself and with this transition and try your best to set the intention to let go of the feelings that arise. Feel the emotions but try not to reject them; set your preference that it will let go naturally.

Jason: I have one more question. There are evolved spirits, spirits of wisdom, etc. What kind of spirit am I?

The Collective: You are typically water, but spirit. You transform into many. Yes, you have different origins; you have one primary base origin, as all souls do. You transform, you ascend, you transcend. It depends on how you're feeling. You're very susceptible to change, you're a friend of receptivity in continuous transformation, you become what is needed for yourself and others, you were a giver of life, and you've taken it away at times.

You create balance, but you don't always have a specific form because of that. It changes depending on what's needed. You have had many lifetimes; you have been many other individuals on many different planets in many different dimensions.

Your third-dimensional world is complicated and can be very harsh, but know that beauty is becoming more robust than ever. Things are changing, and the suffering will end soon; people will reconnect to who they are in the worldly consciousness; people are waking up to have faith.

Jason: I have one more question; I can't explain this level of tenseness in my neck. It just seems like it's so tense. I don't know if something internally is happening to me.

The Collective: Your body is still rejecting third-dimensional life. Even though you signed up for this lifetime; it's very hard on your soul, your spirit, and still, parts of third-dimensional reality don't resonate with you. Your body is fighting what doesn't resonate with you; use acupressure points to help relieve this but understand it will heal once you are fully engaged and happy and resonate with all aspects of your life. That's when it will heal. You can do other things to make it feel better by using different oils, different releasing techniques on the physical body.

And movement will help. Energy can get stuck. Try moving the physical body in ways that resonate releases for the stuck energy, but the stiffness is there to remind you. Suddenly, things are painful, things are challenging, and your body is confused in some ways because of how daily life goes. It is hard to be water and be constricted to a physical body. This is very hard for you; however, you are where you need to be.

Jason: I constantly think of this burst of light coming from my body and this burst of love coming from my heart. I do it regularly, every day. This makes me smile; I continue to smile while trying to stay at a high vibration, this helps me here while incarnated on Earth.

The Collective: Yes, not only does it help you, but it helps everyone else. This energy bursts out far and wide. It's very beneficial for everyone and you.

Jason: Thank you. I have no more questions.

The Collective: Remember to absorb the sun stars. Remember to always set the intention to do it, so you always do well. I send you a hug of light and energy; it is the purest form of unconditional love. We will speak again soon, and I will send you an energy implant.

When you're asleep for the next few days, you may notice different sensations that may happen in your body throughout the next week or even two weeks; try to just acknowledge them and move forward. I'm so glad that we could do this session today.

Jason: I am, too. I guess that's pretty much it. That's all you had planned for me. I'll spend the rest of the day practicing after I'm done with my work—be more within me.

Conversation with Chloe After the Collective Channeling Completed:
Chloe described the healing she received through channeling during my Energy Healing Session. She was connecting to powerful ancestral energy. It felt earthy and connective, but also like it was of a more evolved love state.

Chloe: If the earth was a lot more peaceful, where the inhabitants were a lot more connected and at peace, and where humans were much grounded, centered on the earth, following their missions and passions with full commitment, and being kind to all life- pretty much life respecting- things would have been very different. Because of the imbalance, they kept on surrounding you, sort of in spirit form, and were guiding the entire energy session. I allowed the energy to guide me in methods I'm going to be using, but within this overall method.

The Collective was sending energy to a little version of you. Your energy condensed in my hand, and then I was able to send it more fully, and they did a couple of things that they instructed me to do. The Collective didn't necessarily send energy directly but sent a little bit through me, but they said you need to focus on inspiration.

Inspiration is fundamental. It is necessary for you, for your mission, and it will just help you pretty much in every way of your life. Like, inspiration was a huge theme. Hence, they said it's time for you to be fully integrated into your mission and go head-on into it without any doubts and any worries, and what they said is that you can't think of it mostly logically.

It shouldn't be from the perspective of what people are taught; it's a very realistic and logical step-by-step process. It resides at the other extreme from traditional, so it's important to recognize that you must manifest more and be more tied to your missions and goals. You must be more connected to the energy of inspiration deep within your spirit.

I sent a lot of unconditional love energy, and then they told me to open your heart chakra and surround you with the energy of the heart chakra. Your heart chakra surrounded you like an energy bubble of protection, but it was your energy, and it helped you embody yourself more and made you trust yourself.

It's important not to overthink your mission or why you're here. Follow what feels right and inspire yourself again. This is a huge theme for the entire energy session, and then they sent energy throughout your body, and they asked me if I can connect you to earth with these little nerve endings, almost like roots but a lot gentler. Physical health can be positively impacted due to unconditional love, grounding, and inspiration. Still, it was mostly a theme about embracing and then connecting to these ancestral beings. It seems like they will play a large role in your process moving forward, and they may be very close spirit guides; I can channel more on them.

Jason: When we got into the session, I was trying to figure out what I would ask. I have these small headaches in the back of my head, and it lasted for about a week and just stopped.

Chloe: So, what that reminds me of is, it might be connected in some way cause as soon as you said that, I remembered another portion of the session was about your solar plexus, all the energy besides the heart chakra expanding and surrounding you; it was boosting your solar plexus and basically having your solar plexus in charge. So that could have contributed to your head in some way; people are so used to using their head-mind and using the solar plexus as the main source of energy, and thought could create disruption.

Jason: Who are my spirit guides, and how do I answer them?

Chloe: Answering the spirit; good question. I really think your ancestors are your spirit guides; they didn't tell me how they were connected to you while I was channeling them, but I felt them so strongly connected to you. Let me connect again for you.

The Collective: Where are your ancestral spirit guides? Ancestral spirit guides typically do not relate to the ancestral chain in your current body and current lifetime with family members over the generations. The purpose is to integrate your life mission into your life and embrace that you are close and on the right path. You are embracing the right things. You understand the right concepts, and you must have more confidence in your mission. Sometimes, you get afraid to let go of comfort, stability, and things that have to do with finances and other important components of your 3D life. You'll become more connected and passionate about your mission, and you will just go with the flow of these finances.

When you understand that your actual purpose is to pursue your mission to the best of your abilities, you will find yourself above all worldly desires. You would start waking up at your own pace if you remembered everything; yes, you'd be able to do that. You would also be extremely overwhelmed, and there is a chance that your body would freak out and have a panic attack or a severe heart attack. So, you need some time to rest. You need to relax. You need to be patient and allow the energy to come to you, but all you need to do right now is connect to 5D energy.

5D energy is what's going to manifest these things for you and help you remember, and this is what will bring everything you need into your life. Am I connecting in the same way as I was taught to move forward and help others remember when connected to body energy? Is it through the heart space or is something else absorbing all your precious energy?

Another important part of this process is understanding that grief is an integral part of the change, and belief leads to big changes. People need to learn to listen to their guides because listening is very important. Yes, take your time with this, and don't rush into anything.

The Foundation: Learning How to Consciously and Intentionally Channel

The process of preparation for channeling includes; clearing your energy channel, grounding yourself, raising your vibration, surrendering to love, and trusting yourself and the energy.

There are many methods for the actual channeling process, many of which are shared in Chloe's book on learning how to channel and offered in her online courses. Some of these methods include; Entering the Heart Space, Entering the Heart Portal, Above the Crown, Beside You, and Within Another.

You can find a free online course for learning how to channel on her YouTube channel: Magenta Sun Healing- under the "Playlist Tab." The Playlist is named "Learn How to Channel." Here is the link for her YouTube channel: https://www.youtube.com/@magentasunhealing/playlists. The extended course and book can be purchased on Chloe's website at www.magentasunhealing.com.

Below is a Meditation for Cleansing your Channel from the Book Learn the Art of Channeling by Chloe Moers.

First, rest comfortably by lying or sitting down with your palms facing the sky. Breathe in for a count of 1. 2. 3. 4. Hold for 1. 2. 3. 4. 5. Exhale for a count of 1. 2. 3. 4. 5. 6. Repeat this breathing 3-5 times or however long resonates with you.

Once completed, allow your breathing to rest slightly deeper than it usually is for you and make sure you exhale and inhale fully. Now, share a few words of gratitude and pure genuine love in any way that resonates with you, with source love and all founded from and on source love- including yourself, your higher self, and your spirit guides.

After this is complete, make sure your spine is aligned and as straight as it is able to be in this current moment, and say the following words out loud or within your heart and mind, "I call upon and ask for the brightest and purest of light and the most genuine of source love to connect within and around me with the intention of opening up my energy channel through my chakras and meridian points for the greatest and highest good. I let go and open myself up to receiving this cleansing energy and letting go- allowing all that is not for the greatest and highest good to transform into love."

Now, take a few deep breaths and relax. Allow yourself to let go and truly be present. You may experience various sensations, images, thoughts, and feelings- be with them and be with yourself.

If you feel guided to, you can also visualize this bright light and source of love cleansing your channel and connecting with your being. This is optional.

Allow yourself to rest with the energy for as long as you feel guided. This could be anywhere from 5 minutes to hours.

Once completed, share a few more feelings and words of gratitude and genuine love with source love and light and take a few more deep inhales and exhales, setting your intention moving forward to embrace the most loving of journeys and awakenings.

There are other resources you can connect to for learning the art of conscious channeling, including, but not limited to; Facebook groups, in-person communities and workshops, podcasts, personal meditations, guided meditations, and more. Know that if you learn to access the depths of your being through meditation, you can access all the world's wisdom and beyond from within- including advice and instructions on how to channel consciously.

Remember, the process of channeling can feel, look, and be experienced differently for every individual. Learning how to release fear and trust yourself and the universe is essential. You are a naturally elevated being full of love and joy. You are free to remember yourself and receive the wisdom of life and beyond.

Chapter 10

The Wonders of Astral Projection

Astral projection has been quite an interesting topic for the scientific and general communities. Common questions are about what it is, how it might be practiced, and what benefits might be received. We'll look at these questions and some of the research on the legitimacy of this phenomenon.

What even is Astral Projection? Astral projection, or an out-of-body experience, is a phenomenon in which the consciousness, or astral body, separates from the physical body and travels through the astral plane.

Astral Projection in Pop Culture and History

This type of OBE (out-of-body experience) has often been described during near-death experiences or other traumatic events, so much so that, by this point, it's become something of a cultural shorthand for going through a shocking moment. In fact, in recent years, it's even become a trope that's been seen in popular media, with the likes of the Marvel Cinematic Universe film *Doctor Strange* and the Netflix series *Stranger Things* making use of the concept.

The version they portray is quite similar to the real experience, with their suggestion that through astral projection, an individual can leave their physical body and enter an astral one instead, gaining the ability to travel through the astral planes of existence. In addition to multidimensional travel, the astral projector may also be able to easily travel around the physical world, covering vast distances in an instant and gaining access to information that would otherwise be inaccessible.

Of course, this concept goes back further than some popular movies and TV shows of the 2010s. The term 'astral projection' stretches back to 1875, when it was coined by a group of spiritualists working out of New York City. These spiritualists were drawing on ideas that stretched back to ancient Egypt. According to historians, the ancient Egyptians held the concept of the ka, or astral body, in high regard. In fact, this can even be seen in certain images found in the *Book of the Dead*, images that show the soul, or the ba, as they called it, leaving the body and hovering above it.

Outside of Egypt, other communities and religions have also shown evidence of having some version of an out-of-body experience, with the Judeo-Christian religions even suggesting the concept of the subtle body, or astral body, connected to the physical one via a psychic silver cord. A direct reference to this can be found in the *Book of Ecclesiastes*. It doesn't stop there; Hinduism and Taoism have also given their own examples of this concept in action, as have smaller groups of more isolated indigenous people, such as the Inuit of the Arctic, who share that some of their tribe, known as *angakkuq*, are able to travel to special remote places via a similar process.

With so many cultures around the world having come across the same phenomenon entirely independently of one another, there must be something to it, right? While many have tried to prove that astral projection exists, it has been challenging to prove scientifically, yet many know of its existence.

Astral Projection Across the Ages: Exploring the History and Controversies of Out-of-Body Experiences

Keep in mind that for many centuries there was no proof of germ theory or black holes either, even if today we understand these both to be real phenomena that affect our lives on both micro and cosmic levels. The study of astral projection is what keeps believers focused on proving that the mind can do such things as leave its physical shell. Over the years, this has included the likes of Emanuel Swedenborg, a Swedish philosopher and scientist from the 17th century who wrote extensively about his own out-of-body experiences in his *Spiritual Diary*.

The French novelist Honoré de Balzac would dedicate much of his book, *Luis Lambert*, to the idea that astral experiences exist. Better-known recent figures have also shared these sentiments, with famed activist Helen Keller sharing her experience on astral projection in her book, *My Religion*. In addition, popular novelist Michael Crichton gave some detailed explanations of his own personal experiences with the concept in his nonfiction book, *Travels*.

So, after hundreds of years, there are still many who share of the ability to astral project. To try and gain some more insight into the truth of it all, let's look at how astral projection has been practiced. Let's travel back to the birth of Surat Shabd Simran, a popular meditation and yoga practice developed by the Indian Sant Mat movement during the 13th century.

According to them, astral projection can be achieved through consistent practice of common meditation techniques, such as monitoring breathing and mantra repetition. Many who enter the astral world through meditation will describe themselves as having delved into a deep trance that allows them to focus more easily on their traveling self, the transparent body outside of their physical one.

After they've been able to master this, they might start switching their attention towards looking at their physical body as a separate object, with them finally being able to leave the said body and enter the astral form.

The idea that the astral world and meditation are closely interlinked may come as no surprise to many long-term meditators; at high levels, the relaxation and peace that can be achieved with meditation can feel so exhilarating that it can feel like you're leaving your body and entering some great spiritual realm.

Meditation and out-of-body experiences are connected. Alistair Crowley, an occultist, who practiced the art of leaving his body, achieved this experience by entering trance-like hypnosis states. And once in these states, he would enter a secondary body of light, which he'd previously visualized and discussed in detail in his writings.

This, however, may bring into question the veracity of what he was achieving. Was he leaving his physical body and entering an astral realm, or was he simply in a state of hypnosis, which left him susceptible to believing such things? Skeptics have suggested that while people are experiencing what they believe to be an out-of-body experience, they're unknowingly entering a dream state. And this is, in some ways, backed up by the common Theosophical belief that the astral world and the dream world are the same.

So, wouldn't this mean that we all access it on a nightly basis? Well, according to most scientists, no. It would simply tell that the individual is dreaming and nothing else. Of course, by highlighting this perspective, I don't mean to negate the existence of astral projection. Not at all. I'm trying to search for a scientific basis for the practice. I do this so astral projection will reach a level where mainstream audiences take it more seriously as a potential experience that they might be able to seek out for themselves.

And while this scientific basis has yet to be built, that's not to say it won't be in the future. Take, for example, the idea of dreaming as a link to the astral world. While it may be easy to dismiss this at first glance, to do so would be to disregard the fact that, scientifically speaking, we know very little about the act of dreaming. We don't know why we do it, we don't see how, and we still don't know what our dreams represent (scientifically).

Part of our lack of understanding is that much of the human brain remains a mystery to scientists. It's such a complex organism that many of its secrets will be out of our reach for some time. So, taking this into account, let's consider the idea that by entering an unknown world every night when we close our eyes, a place where the rules of waking logic don't apply and seemingly anything can happen, we're finding ourselves appearing in some other realm.

The idea of different dimensions of existence is now widely regarded as correct, with most scientists believing there are as many as thirteen, nine of which would be outside of human perception- for the most part. But what if we could access some of these other dimensions through our dreams and, if not our dreams directly, through some other meditative state? Again, I'll remind you that we don't know enough about the brain to dismiss this, and that there was a time when the idea of anything outside of the four dimensions of space and time would have seemed ridiculous.

There's tons of evidence to suggest that many people have been able to successfully lucid dream, the practice of recognizing you're in a dream and then, from there, taking control of yourself within it. In fact, there is so much evidence for this being real that most reputable thinkers now accept it as genuine and far more than mere pseudoscience.

Then there is the phenomenon of shared dreams, something many people have reported experiencing with friends and family. You may have even experienced it yourself at some point, seeing someone you know in a dream and having a particular experience, only to then, the next morning, discuss it with them and realize they had the same dream.

Astral Projection: Personal Journeys, Skeptics, and the Power of Trust

In 2014, two Canadian psychologists conducted tests on a twenty-four-year-old woman who claimed to be able to astral project at will. Taking MRI scans of her brain while she was astral traveling, the researchers were able to see that there were changes within her brain patterns consistent with those associated with physical movement, even though she was sitting down at the time.

This suggests that, according to her brain, she was traveling somewhere. Was this an example of her astral body leaving her physical self? The psychologists carrying out the study certainly believe so.

Although, for scientific consensus, it is important to be able to replicate such findings as currently, many scientists don't understand this phenomenon. Bob Bruce of the Queensland Sceptics Association has claimed that the idea of an astral plane doesn't fit in with our current understanding of science and that many of the experiences people claim to have had can be attributed to vivid hallucinations and coincidence.

Perhaps the key phrase to take away from his argument is 'current understanding of science,' as the reality remains that there is much about the universe and ourselves that we don't understand yet. And, for those who know of the existence of astral projection, this is reason enough not to dismiss it.

Unlocking Benefits of Astral Projection

Part of the reason people are so keen to prove that the practice is genuine is because many of them have known of some genuine benefits associated with being able to go through an out-of-body experience. Among these could be the ability to better heal emotionally after a traumatic experience or to overcome the grief of a loved one passing, more easily. And this could be because if astral projection can take us to other planes of existence, you could even find yourself reuniting with a loved one to receive closure.

Additionally, proponents of astral projection find it can be a handy tool in helping people overcome their fears. They'll realize just how small their worries were compared to the magnitude of riches the universe offers them. Whether or not the scientific community agrees on the reality of astral projection is irrelevant, as the experiences people have gone through are real to them, as are the positive aftereffects they experience.

At the very least, there is something undeniably real about astral projection: it has helped many of its practitioners better their lives.

With that said, if you're someone interested in trying astral projection, even if you don't find you're able to do it at first, the very act of trying is a meditative practice, and, in the end, this should help you become a more balanced person, all while further expanding your consciousness in the process. My experiences with astral projection have been helpful and mind-expanding, and I encourage you to explore it and see if it's something you resonate with experiencing.

My First Conscious Astral Projection

One night in the summer of 2020, I was in bed with the intent to leave my body to visit the Akashic Records, but instead, I ended up having an out-of-body experience (OBE). I practiced meditation for weeks to prepare myself for this self-induced experiment I was preparing for.

Once I relaxed, I felt my body fall into a deep trance; my body was asleep, and my mind was awake simultaneously. I felt my arms buzz like an engine was starting up, and then I felt the same sensation in my back, knees, neck, and, eventually, my entire body. Before I knew it, my astral body disengaged from my human avatar, and I floated up into the corner of the room.

I remembered to use mental commands to move my astral body. I wanted to move to the floor, so I thought of this and was close to the floor. I exited the room by thinking of myself behind the door, I was immediately behind my master bedroom door, and into the living room area. From here, I was fully aware, and along with that, I could hear conversations and nature just as clearly as in waking life.

I hovered in my astral body to my middle son's room, who was out of school for summer break. I moved through the door as if it weren't there and observed my son lying with his feet facing the headboard. I watched him on his computer for a second, then shifted to my youngest son's bedroom.

I started thinking about being on the other side of the door, and then I was hovering over my son's bed.

I saw him under the cover doing something on his cell phone; I could see the light beaming through the comforter fabric.

After this OBE, I found myself back in my room, awake and amazed at what just happened. I remember reading in Dr. Monroe's book, *Far Journeys*, that when you return from an OBE, you must write down everything you experienced and then ask questions to the person you observed to validate your experience.

Make sure not to share any details but ask questions in a way that enables you to receive answers to help confirm the legitimacy of your experience. I asked both of my sons what they were doing that late summer night in June of 2020, and they gave the same description I previously mentioned. I was amazed and excited that I had an unplanned out-of-body experience. The fact that I could leave my body and watch my sons in their rooms without them even noticing me for a second is truly unique.

Once I told my boys what happened, they were amazed, and one even wanted to know how he could do it.

Journeying into Astral Projection: Preparation and Persistence

Many astral projectors have stated that it is not an easy achievement and that you must be proficient in deep meditation, which can take years to achieve (depending on the person). So, if you're interested in trying something, be prepared to practice it many times and not get discouraged if it doesn't work immediately. Some have success on their first attempt, and others after their 50th.

But once you finally reach the point where you achieve an out-of-body experience, I suggest focusing on sending yourself to a specific destination- whether this be a place or time in the material world or somewhere otherworldly altogether. This prevents you from aimlessly wandering around, using up valuable psychic energy. Use your time wisely and practice energy cleansing techniques before attempting astral projection- found in this book's chapters on Energy Healing and Channeling.

Mastering Astral Projection: A Comprehensive Step-by-Step Guide

Astral projecting can be a life-changing experience, requiring dedication, practice, trust, letting go, and patience. There are various methods to achieve this experience, not just the one shared below. Here are some basic steps to guide you to an astral project:

1. **Find a quiet, comfortable space:** Choose a location where you won't be disturbed or distracted. Make sure the room temperature is comfortable, and dim the lights to create a relaxing atmosphere.
2. **Rest:** Lay down in a comfortable position, preferably on your back. Ensure your head and body are well supported, and you can relax without feeling any strain.
3. **Relax your body:** Practice progressive muscle relaxation, starting from your toes and gradually moving up through each muscle group until you reach your head. Tense each muscle for a few seconds before slowly releasing it. This process will help you become more aware of your body and release any tension.
4. **Breathe deeply:** Focus on your breath, taking slow, deep breaths. Inhale through your nose and exhale through your mouth. As you breathe, allow your mind to clear and your body to become more relaxed.

5. **Achieve the hypnagogic state:** This is the transitional state between wakefulness and sleep. As you lie there, you may experience sensations such as floating, vibrations or seeing colors and patterns behind your closed eyelids. Maintain awareness during this stage, but avoid getting too excited or anxious, as this can disrupt the process.
6. **Employ the rope technique:** Visualize a rope hanging above your body. In your mind's eye, reach out and grasp the rope with your astral hands and begin to pull yourself up. Focus on the sensation of climbing the rope and feel your astral body rising out of your physical body.
7. **Maintain focus and awareness:** Keep your thoughts and emotions balanced and open as you feel your astral body separating from your physical body. If you feel fearful or overly excited, you may snap back into your physical body, ceasing the experience.
8. **Explore the astral plane:** Once you've successfully separated from your physical body, you can explore the astral plane. Remember that you are in control and can return to your physical body anytime by simply thinking about it.
9. **Re-enter your physical body:** When you're ready to return, focus on your physical body and gently allow your astral body to re-enter it. You can visualize yourself merging if needed. Doing this calmly and smoothly is essential to avoid any disorientation or stress.
10. **Reflect on your experience:** After having an experience in the astral plane, take some time to process and reflect on everything that occurred. You should write down any insights or observations in a journal to help you remember and learn from the journey.

Here is a frequency (found on YouTube) that may assist you on this journey: *Enter the Astral Realm | Binaural Beats Sleep Music for Astral Projection & Out-of-Body Experiences* by the channel, The Lucid Mystic's Sleep Music, https://youtu.be/Jm2XdotYf7E

Many practice practitioners recommend setting the alarm 4-6 hours after you fall asleep initially to attempt the process at this time, as they have noted increased success.

Astral projection can take time and practice to master, so be patient and persistent. Be open to exploring various methods, doing research, following guided meditations, and listening to other people's experiences (this could be through YouTube). With trust and consistent practice, you'll increase your chances of successfully projecting and exploring the astral plane.

Be a Lifelong Learner!

Academic databases such as JSTOR and PubMed can provide access to scholarly articles and research papers related to all the modalities you've explored thus far. These databases compile studies conducted by researchers and experts, offering scientific evidence and analysis to support your understanding of the subjects we've covered and more.

Also, remember the power of your local library or university library. Librarians can guide you to various books, research papers, and resources for each modality we've covered. They can help you locate traditional and contemporary works, providing you with a well-rounded perspective.

In conclusion, your intuition is powerful - so follow it! Flow with the love in your heart and all the wisdom accessible to you through your subconscious mind, the heart, the astral plane, and the Akashic Records. You are one with Source; for this reason, all is already present for remembering.

May you feel freedom in life, light in spirit, love in heart, wisdom in mind, balance in soul, creativity, joy every day, and kindness in connection.

About The Author

Jason Medlock is a highly accomplished mindset and performance coach based in Katy, Texas. With a profound understanding of the human potential and a passion for empowering others, he has dedicated his career to helping business owners, athletes, and everyday working individuals become exceptional leaders capable of achieving their goals with unwavering confidence. Through collaborative and holistic client engagements, Mr. Medlock focuses on strategic personal success, life management, and the elusive art of time management, also known as prioritization.

What sets Mr. Medlock apart is his extraordinary ability to transform businesses from humble beginnings into thriving multimillion-dollar operations. Combining his deep-rooted athletic background with his diverse experience as a successful businessman across various industries, he offers clients insights and strategies that deliver tangible results. At the core of his philosophy lies the firm belief that personal growth is the foundation of success, regardless of the pursuit.

Expansion of Consciousness is an empowering platform that Mr. Medlock created to support people looking to increase their conscious awareness and significantly improve their daily lives because of his own athletic journey and transformative business endeavors. Within this platform, he created Hypnos Awakening, a pioneering approach based on the Quantum Healing Hypnosis Technique (QHHT®) principles. By tapping into their deeper selves—the Higher Self, the Over-Soul, or the Super Conscious—clients gain unparalleled clarity on the reasons behind their life circumstances, enabling them to effect transformative change within themselves.

With an unwavering commitment to personal and spiritual growth, Mr. Medlock embarked on a quest to explore and master various spiritual modalities. Through specialized training with some of the world's foremost spiritual teachers, he has attained certifications as a Remote Viewer, QHHT® Practitioner, Certified Hypnotherapy Practitioner, Master Level Oracle Master, and Certified Level 3 Galactic Energy Healer. Furthermore, his extensive research on astral projection has enriched his understanding of the human experience and expanded his ability to guide others toward their highest potential.

References

Remote Viewing References

Article about 19th-century attempts at remote viewing.
https://eprints.soton.ac.uk/367241/

Article about Joseph Banks Rhine and his experiments
https://sixthsensereader.org/about-the-book/abcderium-index/%E2%80%93-extra-sensory-perception-esp/

Article about Project Stargate
https://papers.ssrn.com/sol3/papers.cfm?abstract_id=3286134

Article or Puthoff and Targ's experiments
https://ciaotest.cc.columbia.edu/olj/sa/sa_jan02srm01.html

Article about experiments on Matthew Manning
https://skepticalinquirer.org/2015/11/poltergeist-scribbler-the-bizarre-case-of-matthew-manning/

Article about Uri Gellar and Rosemary Smith experiments
https://www.warhistoryonline.com/war-articles/project-stargate.html?chrome=1&A1c=1

Jessica Utt's conclusions on Project Stargate
https://web.archive.org/web/20080513174112/http://anson.ucdavis.edu/~utts/air2.html

Ray Hyman's conclusions on Project Stargate
https://web.archive.org/web/20080603202608/http://www.scientificexploration.org/jse/abstracts/v10n1a2.php

Article about how to remote view
https://www.liveabout.com/how-to-experiment-with-remote-viewing-2596363

Article about a remote viewing session
https://www.frieze.com/article/remote-viewing-resurrecting-cias-art-psychic-travel

Astral Projection References

Article about the coining of the term, Astral Projection
https://zenodo.org/record/1039263#.YmFWXVTMK7Q

Egyptian concepts of astral projection
https://docero.net/doc/encyclopedia-of-occultism-parapsychology-melton-5th-ed-vol-2-m-z-kre7722pqy

Judeo-Christian concepts of astral projection
https://bible.oremus.org/?passage=Ecclesiastes%2012:6&version=nrsv

Inuit concepts of astral projection
http://www3.brandonu.ca/cjns/5.2/stott.pdf

Article about Emanuel Swedenborg's thoughts on astral projection
https://swedenborg.com/recap-10-questions-astrology-astral-projection-and-too-much-love/

Luis Lambert by Honoré de Balzac
https://www.gutenberg.org/files/1943/1943-h/1943-h.htm

My Religion by Helen Keller
https://books.google.co.uk/books/about/My_Religion.html?id=x7oPaKrr4x4C

Article about Travels by Michael Crichton
https://www.michaelbonocore.com/2020/05/8-lessons-i-learned-from-reading-travels-by-michael-crichton/36261/

Article about Surat Shabd Simran and astral projection
https://medium.com/sant-mat-meditation-and-spirituality/the-ascension-of-the-soul-into-interior-regions-of-light-sound-part-one-introduction-to-the-4649f4bb06b9

Article about Alestair Crowley and astral projection
https://press.uchicago.edu/Misc/Chicago/642011.html

Article on thirteen dimensions of space/time
https://ui.adsabs.harvard.edu/abs/1988CaJPh..66..292W/abstract

Article on lucid dreaming
https://www.ncbi.nlm.nih.gov/pmc/articles/PMC2737577/

Article on psychedelic drugs and astral projection
https://www.psychologytoday.com/gb/blog/ten-zen-questions/202005/psychedelics-and-the-out-body-experience

The experiences of an astral projector
https://www.bustle.com/life/how-to-experience-astral-projection-astrologer-psychic

Article about MK Ultra
https://www.vice.com/en/article/pad4a9/the-us-army-funded-astral-projection-and-hypnosis-research-in-the-80s

2014 research paper
https://www.frontiersin.org/articles/10.3389/fnhum.2014.00070/full

Video on the benefits of astral projection
https://www.facebook.com/watch/?v=1222642871592700

Meditation References

Religious uses of meditation
https://www.news-medical.net/health/Meditation-Spirituality-and-Religion.aspx#:~:text=Meditation%20can%20be%20used%20as

Health benefits of meditation
https://www.healthline.com/nutrition/12-benefits-of-meditation
https://www.nccih.nih.gov/health/meditation-in-depth
https://health.ucdavis.edu/news/headlines/10-health-benefits-of-meditation/2019/06

Info about transcendental meditation
https://uk.tm.org/

Info about Headspace
https://www.headspace.com/meditation-101/what-is-meditation

2014 US National Center for Complementary and Integrative Health review
https://www.ncbi.nlm.nih.gov/pmc/articles/PMC4142584/

2017 American Heart Association report
https://www.ncbi.nlm.nih.gov/pmc/articles/PMC5721815/

MRI and EEG reports suggesting health benefits
https://www.sciencedirect.com/science/article/abs/pii/S0149763414000724?via%3Dihub

Benefits of meditation in the workplace
https://hbr.org/2015/12/why-google-target-and-general-mills-are-investing-in-mindfulness

Potential risks of meditation
https://www.psychologytoday.com/us/blog/mindfulness-wellbeing/201603/dangers-meditation

Psychedelics References

Article about psychedelics
https://www.ncbi.nlm.nih.gov/pmc/articles/PMC4813425/

Further information about specific psychedelics
https://www.verywellmind.com/types-of-psychedelic-drug-22073

Mescaline usage among Indigenous Americans
https://www.researchgate.net/publication/7754322_Prehistoric_peyote_use_Alkaloid_analysis_and_radiocarbon_dating_of_archaeological_specimens_of_Lophophora_from_Texas

Psilocybin usage amongst African tribes
https://link.springer.com/referenceworkentry/10.1007/978-94-007-6728-7_6-2

Article on legal status of psychedelics
https://psychedelicspotlight.com/why-are-psychedelics-illegal/

Article about racial implications behind Cannabis criminalisation

https://www.businessinsider.com/racist-origins-marijuana-prohibition-legalization-2018-2?r=US&IR=T

Article about Staggers-Dodd bill
https://mrpsychedeliclaw.com/history/

Convention on Psychotropic Substances of 1971 report
https://treaties.un.org/pages/ViewDetails.aspx?src=TREATY&mtdsg_no=VI-16&chapter=6

Article about psychedelics and MK Ultra
https://www.npr.org/2019/09/09/758989641/the-cias-secret-quest-for-mind-control-torture-lsd-and-a-poisoner-in-chief

Article about Timothy Leary
https://www.newyorker.com/books/under-review/the-science-of-the-psychedelic-renaissance

Article about Johns Hopkins Medicine being awarded funding to do research into psychedelics
https://www.hopkinsmedicine.org/news/newsroom/news-releases/johns-hopkins-medicine-receives-first-federal-grant-for-psychedelic-treatment-research-in-50-years

Article about therapeutic use of psychedelics
https://www.ncbi.nlm.nih.gov/pmc/articles/PMC4592297/

Article about short and long term effects of psychedelics on the brain
https://nida.nih.gov/publications/drugfacts/hallucinogens

Article about reasons for legalization of psychedelics
https://www.vox.com/2015/7/24/9027363/acid-lsd-psychedelic-drugs

Article about Ketamine's use as an antidepressant
https://www.ncbi.nlm.nih.gov/pmc/articles/PMC7225830/

Article on safe usage of psychedelics
https://psyche.co/guides/how-to-have-a-safe-psychedelic-trip

Article about benefits of psychedelics on cancer patients and addicts
https://www.medicalnewstoday.com/articles/psychedelic-therapy#uses-and-benefits

Article about decriminalization of psychedelics
https://www.pbs.org/newshour/politics/why-the-push-to-decriminalize-psychedelics-is-growing-in-michigan

Article about addictiveness of psychedelics
https://www.medicalnewstoday.com/articles/are-psychedelics-addictive-side-effects-and-risks

Article on ego death
https://www.mindbodygreen.com/articles/ego-death

Manifestation References

1. https://parade.com/1065715/leighweingus/manifestation-definition/
2. https://www.vox.com/the-goods/21524975/manifesting-does-it-really-work-meme

3. https://selfpause.com/manifestation/where-does-manifestation-originate/
4. https://www.mentalhelp.net/blogs/the-science-of-manifestation/#:~:text=The%20science%20behind%20manifestation%20pertains,to%20successfully%20achieve%20their%20goals.
5. A Guide to Manifesting a Compassionate World (book) by Chloe Moers
6. https://www.capitalfm.co.ke/thesauce/five-amazing-benefits-of-manifestation-in-your-life/
7. https://www.integrativenutrition.com/blog/how-to-manifest
8. facebook.com/groups/themyhmanifestationcommunity/
9. https://www.silkandsonder.com/blogs/news/5-manifestation-exercises-to-help-you-get-exactly-what-you-want-in-2022
10. https://www.techtarget.com/whatis/definition/quantum-theory

Hypnosis References

1. https://science.howstuffworks.com/science-vs-myth/extrasensory-perceptions/hypnosis1.htm
2. https://instituteofclinicalhypnosis.com/hypnosis/history-of-hypnosis/
3. https://positivepsychology.com/hypnotherapy/#:~:text=A%20fascinating%20study%20in%202006,%2C%20%26%20Laureys%2C%202006).
4. https://med.stanford.edu/news/all-news/2016/07/study-identifies-brain-areas-altered-during-hypnotic-trances.html
5. https://www.independent.co.uk/life-style/the-dangers-of-memory-can-regression-therapy-by-hypnosis-produce-false-recollections-of-sexual-abuse-hester-lacey-reports-5431250.html
6. https://rtt.com/how-to-hypnotize-someone/
7. https://general-hypnotherapy-register.com/
8. https://www.professionalstandards.org.uk/check-practitioners/practitioner/hypnotherapist

9. https://www.mayoclinic.org/tests-procedures/hypnosis/about/pac-20394405#:~:text=Hypnosis%20is%20a%20changed%20state,people%20feel%20calm%20and%20relaxed.
10. https://www.rcpsych.ac.uk/mental-health/treatments-and-wellbeing/hypnosis-and-hypnotherapy
11. https://www.healthline.com/health/mental-health/self-hypnosis#how-to-try

The Subconscious Mind References

1. https://imotions.com/blog/learning/research-fundamentals/what-is-the-subconscious-mind/
2. https://www.ncbi.nlm.nih.gov/pmc/articles/PMC2440575/
3. https://www.simplypsychology.org/unconscious-mind.html
4. https://www.nature.com/articles/srep08478
5. https://eocinstitute.org/meditation/subconscious-mind-power-2/
6. https://www.forbes.com/sites/briannawiest/2018/09/12/13-ways-to-start-training-your-subconscious-mind-to-get-what-you-want/?sh=1e45b7c7d69f
7. https://www.apa.org/pubs/journals/cns
8. https://www.bps.org.uk/research-digest/feeling-hungry-better-let-your-subconscious-make-decisions
9. https://inlpcenter.org/subconscious-mind/
10. https://tellmethegoodnews.com/subconscious-mind-exercises/

Share Your Empowered Experience with Us!

Spread some positivity our way!

- We're eager to hear how Empowered by Consciousness has impacted you and led to your breakthrough moments. Feel free to share your stories; we'll keep the conversation going.
- Leaving a review on platforms like Amazon or wherever you got your copy of Empowered by Consciousness would mean the world to us.
- Stay connected and stay in the loop by following us on social media and checking out our website.

Your support means everything to us!

HOW TO GET IN TOUCH

- WEBSITE – www.JasonMedlock.com
- AUTHOR EMAIL – jason@jasonmedlock.com
- PUBLIC EMAIL – info@jasonmedlock.com

CONNECT SOCIALLY WITH JASON

- FACEBOOK – www.facebook.com/EXPANSIONOFCONSCIOUS
- TWITTER – twitter.com/EXPANSIONOFCON
- INSTAGRAM – www.instagram.com/expansionofconscious/
- LINKEDIN – www.linkedin.com/in/expansionofconsciousness/
- YOUTUBE – www.youtube.com/@expansionofconsciousness
- TIKTOK – www.tiktok.com/@expansionofconsciousness

Subscribe to our YouTube show Expansion of Consciousness the Podcast
www.youtube.com/@expansionofconsciousness

"Embark on a Transformative Journey with
Our Dynamic Courses.
Discover the Life-Changing Path to Exploring Hypnosis
and Mastering Your Subconscious Mind."

Sign Up Today at:
www.JasonMedlock.com

More ways to enhance your mindset with our thought-provoking courses!

Have you heard of the Quantum Healing Hypnosis Technique℠? It's a captivating journey that explores the depths of your mind, body, and spirit. This technique is practiced globally and is sought out by individuals for various reasons, such as relieving physical discomfort, gaining clarity in their life journey, satisfying their curiosity, or connecting with their Higher Self. It is a profound experience that expands the soul and heals the heart.

Welcome to the "Transform Your Mindset Boot Camp," where you will embark on a profound personal growth and empowerment journey. Over seven intense days, we will guide you through powerful lessons, immersive hypnosis sessions, and transformative exercises to help you break free from limiting beliefs and unlock your true potential.

Are you ready to embark on a life-changing journey of self-discovery and empowerment? Introducing "Elevate Your Mindset: A 12-Week Empowerment Intensive," a transformative program designed to help you break free from self-doubt, overcome limitations, and unlock your true potential. Imagine a life where you wake up daily feeling inspired, confident, and driven to achieve your goals. Envision yourself stepping into your power, conquering fears, and easily manifesting your dreams. This is the reality that awaits you in Elevate Your Mindset.

Made in the USA
Middletown, DE
24 October 2023

41308506R00119